My Father,
the Pornographer

ALSO BY CHRIS OFFUTT

The Same River Twice

No Heroes

Out of the Woods

The Good Brother

Kentucky Straight

My Father,
the Pornographer

A Memoir

Chris Offutt

ATRIA BOOKS

NEW YORK   LONDON   TORONTO   SYDNEY   NEW DELHI

ATRIA BOOKS

An Imprint of Simon & Schuster, Inc.
1230 Avenue of the Americas
New York, NY 10020

First Atria Books hardcover edition February 2016

ATRIA B O O K S and colophon are trademarks of Simon & Schuster, Inc.

For information about special discounts for bulk purchases, please contact Simon & Schuster Special Sales at 1-866-506-1949 or business@simonandschuster.com.

The Simon & Schuster Speakers Bureau can bring authors to your live event. For more information, or to book an event, contact the Simon & Schuster Speakers Bureau at 1-866-248-3049 or visit our website at www.simonspeakers.com.

Interior design by Kyoko Watanabe

Manufactured in the United States of America

10 9 8 7 6 5 4 3 2 1

Library of Congress Cataloging-in-Publication Data

Offutt, Chris.
 My father, the pornographer : a memoir / Chris Offutt.
    pages cm
1. Offutt, Chris. 2. Offutt, Chris—Family. 3. Novelists, American—20th century—Family relationships. 4. Novelists, American—20th century—Biography. 5. Fathers and sons—United States. 6. Pornography—United States. I. Title.
 PS3565.F387Z474 2016
 813'.54—dc23
 [B]
                   2015027503

ISBN 978-1-5011-1246-1
ISBN 978-1-5011-1248-5 (ebook)

Excerpts of this book have appeared in *The New York Times Magazine*, *River Teeth*, *The Best American Essays*, *Zoetrope*, and *Jelly Bucket*.

DEDICATED TO

Andrew Jefferson Offutt V
John Cleve
Turk Winter
Jeff Morehead
Jay Andrews
Opal Andrews
Drew Fowler
J. X. Williams
Jack Cory
Jeremy Crebb
John Denis
Alan Marshall
Jeff Woodson
Joe Brown
Jeff Douglas
Roscoe Hamlin
Camille Colben
Anonymous

As John Cleve, I will be famous in the next century. Bet on it.

—ANDREW J. OFFUTT, 1978

If not for writing pornography, I'd have been a serial killer.

—ANDREW J. OFFUTT, 1986

My Father,
the Pornographer

Chapter One

MY FATHER grew up in a log cabin near Taylorsville, Kentucky. The house had twelve-inch walls with gun ports to defend against attackers, first Indians, then soldiers during the Civil War. At age twelve, Dad wrote a novel of the Old West. He taught himself to type with the Columbus method—find it and land on it—using one finger on his left hand and two fingers on his right. Dad typed swiftly and with great passion. He eventually wrote and published more than four hundred books under eighteen different names. His novels included six science fiction, twenty-four fantasy, and one thriller. The rest was pornography.

When I was nine, Dad gave me his childhood copy of *Treasure Island* by Robert Louis Stevenson. The old hardback was tattered, the boards held by fraying strips of fabric, the pages pliant and soft. It is a coming-of-age narrative about thirteen-year-old Jim Hawkins, who discovers a secret map, leaves England, and returns with a large share of pirate treasure. I loved the fast-paced story and the bravery of young Jim.

On paper cut from a brown grocery sack, I carefully drew an

island with a coastline, water, and palm trees. A dotted line led to a large red X. My mother suggested I show the map to my father. Dad wiped coffee on the paper and wadded it up several times, which made it seem older. He used matches to ignite the edges of the map, then quickly extinguished the flame. This produced a charred and ragged border that enhanced the map's appearance, as if it had barely survived destruction. Because of the fire involved, we were alone outside, away from my younger siblings. Dad was selling insurance at the time, rarely home, his attention always focused elsewhere. I enjoyed the sense of closeness, a shared project.

Dad said that he drew maps for most of the books he wrote, and I resolved that if I ever published a book, I'd include a map. Twenty years later I did. In 1990 I called my father with the news that Vintage Contemporaries was publishing *Kentucky Straight*, my first book. A long silence ensued as Dad digested the information.

"I'm sorry," he said.

"What do you mean?" I said.

"I didn't know I'd given you a childhood terrible enough to make you a writer."

His own father wrote short stories in the 1920s. During the Depression, my grandfather was forced to abandon his literary ambitions to save the family farm and pursue a more practical education in engineering. He died young, a year before my father published his first story. Dad never knew what it was like to have a proud father and didn't know how to be one himself.

After the publication of *Kentucky Straight*, people began asking Dad what he thought of my success. Buried in the question was the implication that the son had outdone the father. My work was regarded as serious literature, whereas he wrote porn and science fiction. Twice I witnessed someone insinuate that Dad should be envious. Invariably my father had the same response. His favorite adventure novel was *The Three Musketeers*, in which young

D'Artagnan wins respect through his magnificent swordplay, taught to him by his father. Every time someone asked Dad about my success as a writer, he said he was happy to be D'Artagnan's sword master, voicing pride in my accomplishments but taking credit for them, as well. It was as close as he ever came to telling me how he felt about my work.

Chapter Two

MY FATHER was a brilliant man, a true iconoclast, fiercely self-reliant, a dark genius, cruel, selfish, and eternally optimistic. Early in his sales career, a boss called him an "independent son of a bitch," which Dad took as the highest compliment he'd ever received. He wanted me to be the same way.

Dad had no hobbies, no distractive activities. He didn't do household chores, wash the car, mow the grass, go shopping, or fix anything. He never changed a lightbulb. I never saw him hold a screwdriver, stand on a ladder, or consult a repair manual. His idea of cleaning was to spit on a tissue and wipe the object. He didn't sleep much. He drank. He rarely left the house. Dad was an old-school pulp writer, a machine who never stopped. In his home office hung a handmade sign that said: "Writing Factory: Beware of Flying Participles."

The winter of 1968 was known in the hills as "the year of the big snows," which closed my grade school for two weeks and trapped the family on our home hill in eastern Kentucky. For the first time in my father's life, he could do what he always wanted—write fourteen hours a day. He ran out of cigarettes and Mom sent me to the general store a couple of miles away. I followed a path through the woods, each leafless tree limb lined with a layer of white. Frozen deer saliva glistened at the ends of chewed branches.

I made good time by walking the iced-over creek, sliding my feet along the bright surface. Smoke from the store's wood stove rose to the top of the ridge, then flattened and began to dissipate in a long, low ribbon. Inside I sat by the fire until my wet pants legs were steaming and my feet had warmed. The proprietor, a kind man named George, gave me a piece of chocolate. He'd been in operation since the forties, the only business to survive the closing of the mines. He sold me cigarettes and I went home.

The following week I walked to the bootlegger for Dad. I left our dirt road for a game path through the woods, staying high enough on the hill to evade dogs. After a mile I dropped down the hill and crossed the blacktop to the bootlegger's small shack. It was a one-room building with a sliding plywood panel serving as a window. No one ever robbed it, a testament to local respect and fear. I stood on layers of snow packed hard from tire tracks and the tread of many boots. The man inside was red-faced, with wild hair.

"Whose boy are you?" he said in a gruff voice.

"Andy Offutt's first boy," I said. "Chris."

"Offutt," he said. "Uh-huh. What's he wanting?"

"Bourbon."

"Bourbon," he said. "Yep. Reckon you're his boy, then."

I placed ten dollars on the rough wood shelf. He exchanged the money for two pints of whiskey. I reached for them, but he grabbed my wrist with a grip stronger than I'd ever felt, as if the bones were rasping inside my arm. It was a test of sorts, and I tried not to show pain.

"Don't you ever fuck with me," he said.

I shook my head obediently. He released me and I entered the woods. Concealed from view, I dropped to my knees and rubbed snow on my wrist until both hands were numb. I could feel tears frozen below my eyes and was embarrassed, even alone in the ivory silence.

One summer a few years later, my two best friends and I decided we'd try drinking. We met at night in the woods and walked to the bootlegger. A different man was there, legendary for the length of his tongue, a .357 Magnum he occasionally flashed, and a certain rough charm with women. I told him I was Andy Offutt's first boy and he'd sent me for whiskey. My buddies each bought what their fathers drank, and we left with bourbon, a half case of beer, and a large bottle of cheap red wine. Undoubtedly the bootlegger knew we were lying, but the hills were lawless in the 1960s.

We resorted to walking the blacktop, which would take less time than traversing the woods. The road curved three hundred yards to the top of a hill, then a long slow drop to the creek. We lightened our load by drinking a beer. I hated the taste and switched to whiskey. We headed down the hill. By the time we reached the bottom, I'd finished one half-pint and opened another, then fell in the creek and took a rest. I woke up in a car and went back to sleep. Next I awakened sick to my stomach on the front porch of a nearby house. I made it home and went to bed. It was a disgraceful beginning to the pleasures of alcohol, a clear warning to stay away from whiskey. Instead, I visited the bootlegger dozens of times before leaving Kentucky. Drinking bourbon changed the terrible way I consistently felt about myself. I suppose it was the same for Dad, who eventually died of liver failure.

And the boys I got drunk with that first time forty years ago? One shot himself to death and the other will be released from prison at age seventy-five.

Chapter Three

BY 2012 Dad had been occupying a large chair for several years, eating, sleeping, drinking, and writing there. Three days before Christmas my mother called my house in Mississippi, a rarity in itself. She spoke rapidly, her voice fraught with anxiety, an element of despair coursing beneath her words. I'd never heard this tone from her. She informed me that my father had fallen. Too small to help him up, Mom had called an ambulance service. The EMTs took Dad to the hospital, where the doctors decided to keep him. Mom wasn't sure why.

"Would you please come home?" she said.

The nature of our family is that no one appeals for help of any kind—not financial, emotional, or moral support. Since Mom was asking, I knew it was serious. Uncertain of the circumstances, I packed clothes appropriate to a funeral, drove all day, and arrived on the winter solstice, gray and rainy, a sense of melancholy draping the hills. I went straight to the hospital. Dad was too bloated for diagnosis. The first order of business was draining forty pounds of fluid, which wasn't going well.

I accompanied Mom to the house in which I'd grown up, her home of fifty years. My mother loved Dad with a tenacious loyalty and devotion. She accepted his quirks and admired his brilliance. The strength of their marriage was due solely to her. She ran every errand, shopped, cooked, cleaned, and drove her children places. She typed every final manuscript Dad wrote.

Mom was five feet, two inches tall, with red hair, green eyes, and a good figure. She stayed out of the sun to avoid freckling. For a year after high school she attended Transylvania University, left for economic reasons, and began working in a bank. She'd always regretted not furthering her education, and in 1980 she enrolled at Morehead State University, where I was a senior. For the next twelve years she took a few classes per year as one of the first continuing education students at MSU, receiving a BA in philosophy and a master's in English. She taught freshman composition for three years on campus, then began teaching at the newly opened state prison in West Liberty, Kentucky.

From ages sixty-five to seventy-eight, she worked full-time as a secretary in Morehead to supplement their combined Social Security income. Mom was adamant that they didn't need the money, but I understood the truth—my parents' sense of pride forbade her from admitting financial need. I also know that the job was crucial in that it provided my mother with escape five days a week. Her children had left home and moved far away, but Mom could get only as far as the nearest town for work. She had her own life there—walking to the bank every day, chatting with the mailman and a woman who worked at the liquor store.

The morning after I arrived home, Mom rose early and went to the hospital. I walked through the house and discovered that two weeks of heavy rain had flooded the basement, which was not draining. Dad had always called his neighbor Jimmy to deal with plumbing problems. Jimmy was dead, so I called his son, who showed up promptly. Sonny and I were glad to see each other but stood awkwardly in the drizzling rain, unsure what to do. Men in the hills didn't touch except to punch each other or accidentally brush arms while engaged in a shared chore. We grinned and looked away, scratched ourselves, and grinned some more. I asked how he was, and he said, "Straight as a stick, son."

The water in the basement was six inches deep, more than Sonny or I had ever seen there. I'd brought shoes suitable for the woods but not wading and remained on the basement steps with a flashlight. Sonny moved slowly through the water, seeking the drain, wearing large rubber boots. He said they'd belonged to his dad. At the top of the steps I found my father's old zip galoshes. The rubber was ripped at the stress marks across the toe. I wrapped two plastic bags around my feet and slid them into Dad's boots.

Sonny was crouching over the drain. He dipped his hand into the murky water, felt around briefly, and said: "Phillips." I went upstairs and fetched a Phillips-head screwdriver. Sonny removed the drain cap and fed the metal snake into the pipe. I remembered being a child and watching Jimmy snake out the drain while Dad stood idly by, holding a flashlight. Now Sonny and I repeated their behavior, wearing our fathers' boots.

The walls of the basement were moldy, the rafters covered in cobwebs. Dark water moved beneath our feet. The motor rattled as the steel wire coiled and uncoiled within the drum. I recalled playing in the basement with Sonny and his brothers. As the youngest boy on the hill, he trailed behind us and never spoke. I mentioned the past to Sonny, but he had no interest in nostalgia. He was occupying the moment, running the snake by feel, staring into the middle distance, frowning and muttering exactly as his father had. Sonny believed the snake was getting diverted into another pipe. He retracted it and tried again.

"Still writing tales?" he said.

I told him yes and he nodded once, returning his attention to the snake. Very few of the boys I grew up with had finished high school, but they accepted that I was a writer. I was merely doing what other men did—following in my father's footsteps. Sonny was a plumber. The son of a local drunk was the town drunk in two towns. Sons of soldiers joined the army. That I had become a writer was perfectly normal.

The water level lapped against the walls from our movement. One of Dad's boots began to leak. Sonny shut off the machine. He told me to go down the hill twenty-five feet to the old sewage trench, now replaced by a septic tank. As a kid I'd spent hundreds of hours over the hill, finding snakeskins and rabbit dens, old bottles and animal bones, feathers and lucky rocks. I knew the gap in the brush and the best route down. In the forty years since my last venture, bushes had spread and grown, and I was much less agile. My boot skidded and I went to one knee but remained upright. Rooted in earth rich with human waste, the forsythia tendrils were higher than my head, bigger than my thumb, tangled and knotted together. Rain fell in waves. I had no hat or gloves.

Facing a row of briars, I knew instinctively to rotate my body into them, letting the thorns scrape but not grab hold. Now I had to find the old sewage trench. The rain increased. I crawled beneath the heavy overhang, moving slowly, joints stiff, the weight of my body hurting my hands pressed to the ground. Sonny yelled from the top of the hill. I couldn't see him, but I waved my arms and shook a bush. He wanted to know if I heard anything.

"What am I supposed to hear?" I said.

"Anything, son. Listen at the ground. It's not supposed to make no noise, so anything you hear is good."

He went back in the house. The rain slackened momentarily. I bent forward and cupped my ears toward the earth. I heard cars on the blacktop at the foot of the hill and the gentle sound of thousands of raindrops striking thousands of leaves. I heard my own ragged breathing.

After a few minutes, Sonny yelled for me to come back to the house. The bushes were too intertwined for me to stand upright, and I had to scuttle backward. Limbs scratched my skin. Water ran into my pants. I emerged into a small clearing and tugged my clothes in place, shivering from the cold and sweating from exertion. I took two steps, slipped, and fell. Mud spattered my glasses. My cell phone rang and I ignored it. I fell twice more, scraping my hands. A branch tore along my cheek. I was breathing hard. It occurred to me that if I had a heart attack, Sonny would drag me up the hill and drive me to the hospital. Maybe I'd share a room with Dad.

I regained the safety of the yard. Sonny had packed up his snake machine and said he'd come back later and look for another drain. I was wet and muddy, irritated at the world and myself. Only a damn fool plunges down a steep hill, out of shape at age fifty-four, and attempts to hear the sound of dirt. I listened to the voicemail on my phone. The doctor thought my father might need a transfusion and my blood type matched his. I told Sonny, who looked away, then spoke quietly: "You need you a ride to the hospital?"

I shrugged and he said to get in. The sun was going down. We talked of our varied marriages, old buddies, and grade school teachers. Sonny dropped me at the hospital, but the medical emergency turned out be premature. Dad's condition had stabilized. The catheter had begun draining.

Late that evening, the water was gone from the basement. I called Sonny, who said he'd found a better clean-out drain against the wall closest to the hill. He suggested I write its location on the wall in case someone else came next time. Sonny's idea was practical and smart, but it shocked me. The notion of writing on the wall, even a dim basement corner, was unthinkable. It violated Dad's rules. You wrote on pieces of paper, organized them into a manuscript, and produced a book. You didn't write on a wall any more than you would spit on the floor. But Dad was sick and I was Sonny's assistant. I had my instructions.

In the corner, I found the correct drain that led to the septic tank. I removed the cap of a black marker, its sharp scent momentarily overpowering the mold. In my life I've written over ten million words, but never before on a wall. If Dad found out, he wouldn't like it, and I'd get in trouble. In large letters I wrote "Clean-Out Drain" with an arrow pointing down.

At the foot of the steps, I glanced around the muddy basement one more time. I'd spent a lot of time down here, especially during winter, when school was canceled from snow. Now it was full of old Tupperware, empty beer bottles, and rotting wood. A rusty metal shelf held canned food that had expanded, the paper labels chewed by mice. I remembered killing a snake in a corner, then setting mousetraps for months.

Sonny had done a good job. He'd emptied the basement with more efficiency than the doctors had drained fluid from my father. Briefly, I imagined Sonny as a doctor—his bedside manner was gentle, and he'd have a nurse to retrieve tools instead of me.

I went outside in the chilly darkness. The rain had quit. Water dripped from leaves. An owl moaned along the ridge. The storm had cleared the sky, revealing the same swath of stars I looked at as a child. I listened intently. It occurred to me that the silence I heard was the sound of dirt.

Chapter Four

THE DOCTOR diagnosed my father with alcohol-induced cirrhosis and gave him six months to live. I arranged for a man to build a wheelchair ramp next to the driveway. I was proud of myself. I couldn't help my father, but I could make it easy for him to get in and out of the house. He came home and returned to his chair. I went back to Mississippi.

The past decade had been difficult for me, beginning with the blow of divorce. Instead of writing, I'd devoted myself to my sons: shopping, cooking, cleaning, doing laundry, and driving them around. A few years later I married Melissa Ginsburg, a poet from Texas, and soon faced a fresh dilemma: My teenage sons wanted to go to college, and I was broke and unemployed. To finance their education, I taught myself screenwriting and worked on three television shows, *True Blood, Weeds,* and *Treme.* Hollywood was a world into which I never fully fit, beginning with my fear of driving in Los Angeles. Still, I blundered along, doing my best, living in hotels and furnished apartments for a few months at a time. I stayed focused on my plan—get the money and get out. After my sons went to college, I took a permanent position at the University of Mississippi and rented an old house seven miles from town.

The first summer in Mississippi, before Dad got sick, I drove home to see my parents, the only time in my life I visited them alone. Prior to that, other family members had been present, or my wife and sons had accompanied me. I stayed in Morehead at a motel on the interstate because Dad made it clear that I was welcome only after four o'clock in the afternoon. He implied that it was related to his work, since he was still writing, but the timing turned out to revolve around his schedule for drinking. Dad told me he was the happiest man in the world. The only complaint he had was the weekends, because Mom was in the house. They got along fine, that wasn't the problem. Her presence interfered with his solitude, as did my visit.

Six months later he was dying, and I called regularly. He had already survived a massive heart attack, two minor strokes, and numerous lesser ailments. A smoker for forty years, he was permanently tethered to an oxygen tank for COPD. Dad always believed he'd die young, as his own father had. He was surprised to make it to age forty-five, then fifty, sixty, seventy, and seventy-five. Now his body was running down. In the last month of his illness, Dad knew death was near. He fell asleep on the phone, woke up, repeated what he'd just said, and was angry for doing so. An escalation of the pattern rankled him.

"I think, son, it's the beginning of the end."

"Might be," I said.

"Probably is."

"Probably so."

"Maybe not," he said.

The conversation contained a familiar tinge of conflict, and I resolved to go along with anything he said. In the end, death reduced every dispute to a draw.

He talked of his childhood, of the farm his father fought to save in the Depression, and how the land went to Uncle Johnny.

"Who's that?" I asked.

"My father's brother."

"You never talked about him."

"Why would I? He got the farm. He never worked it. Dad and I did, but Uncle Johnny got it. I never saw him again."

"What was he like?"

"Why do you care about him? I'm dying, not him."

He had a point, a good one. But it was astonishing to hear about a relative I'd never met. Uncle Johnny's grandsons would be close to my age. I wondered if they knew about our family, about me.

"I'm not afraid of this," Dad said. "I don't want you to think I'm trying to put on a fake front. I'm really not. If the pain gets bad, I've got a half a bottle of Percocet hidden. I'll take them with whiskey. If the pain gets bad."

"I understand."

"Your mother knows. I told her."

"It's a backup plan," I said. "Doesn't mean you'll do it."

There was a long gap in our conversation. He spoke again.

"It surprises me that I'm not afraid. I had a pretty good run. Now I'll find out if there really is an afterlife. Or if it's just a long rest that I won't know about. It's hard to think of the world without me being in it."

There are times in people's lives when a significant event occurs and they're not aware of it—the last time you pick up a son before he's too heavy, the final kiss of a marriage gone bad, the view of a beloved landscape you'll never see again. Weeks later, I realized those were Dad's last words to me.

The day he died, I drove home a final time. The highway unfurled before me as if the car were a time capsule bent on depositing me in the past. I didn't like how I felt because I didn't feel anything.

I hadn't cried. I was aware solely of the burden of responsibility—firstborn, eldest son, head of the family.

Dad's mother died in 1984. He was fifty years old, had outlived both his parents. The sense of feeling orphaned led him to address his own mortality by composing a legal will, which he sent to my siblings and me. The terms were simple—everything went to Mom. If they died together, the rest of us split the estate equally four ways.

Included with the will was a long meandering letter that referred to silver and gold hidden in the house. For two pages he discussed his relationship with the first Macintosh computer on the market, delighted at his own skill at modifying fonts and learning to program it on his own. He closed with instructions that he'd appointed me to deal with the contents of his office.

> *On you Chris, I decided, this task and onus must fall—and I'm telling the others this without the reason. The examination of the office and disposal of its contents is totally up to Christopher J. Offutt, and this is oh-fficial.*

In a separate envelope with a return address of General Douglas MacArthur, Dad sent me a secret will that furthered the details of the public version. He included instructions about his porn, where it was hidden and what to do with it. An accompanying letter expressed his reasons for not involving my siblings—he evaluated each in a petty manner and found them all lacking. I immediately wrote to my brother and sisters, offering a copy of the secret will to alleviate any concern that I might be receiving special favor. They demurred, already bored by porn and weary of his secrecy.

The secret will explained Dad's long interest in pornography. The major difference between his own books and current writers was attitude:

They obviously dislike women, or worse, and I've always
been crazy about 'em. I am not a sadist: I have sadistic
tendencies. That difference is enormous.

He expressed his preference for porn from the Victorian era and
his reverence for the Marquis de Sade, who wrote detailed sexual
fantasies while in prison. Dad lamented recent changes in the mar-
ketplace while firmly affixing his own status:

Pornography is not what it was in my day. Both bondage
& torture pix and descriptions have become more violent
& obscene. Publishers get what they pay for: garbage.
*   I was The Class Operator in that field, Christopher*
J., & there will be no successor.

The letter ends with a fierce exhortation that I not cross him
up by getting killed. If so, he'd have to come barrelling up to my
Boston apartment and try to find this very letter.

I'd become accustomed to unusual letters from Dad. Often
they carried the signature of "John Cleve." The name began as a
pseudonym for porn but developed into a full persona when I was
a child. Cleve's signature differed greatly from the others. It was
less formal, with joyously looping letters that ended in a circle with
an arrow—the symbol for being male, the planet Mars, and the
chemical element of iron. Letters from John Cleve were filled with
provocative comments about women, ebullient use of punctuation,
and humorous wordplay.

In later years, I received an occasional missive signed by Turk
Winter, the persona who eventually replaced John Cleve. Turk's
signature was equally stylized, with a horizontal line that crossed
both T's and flared upward. There was an intensity to the smallness
of the signature, the individual letters legible and terse.

Though I searched the letters for clues, I could never quite discern a reason for the differing signatures. It didn't seem related to content. I concluded that it was the personality he was embodying, or perhaps that embodied him. After I left home, the varying signatures were the first indication I had that explained my father's drastic and sudden shifts in mood when I was a child. Arbitrary rules changed abruptly, with swift consequences for breaking them. It's possible that each persona viewed his domain with different expectations and decrees. None of us knew whom we were dealing with at any given moment.

Of nearly two hundred letters I received from my father, only one was unsigned—the one that accompanied the secret will. The absence of authorial attribution lent greater credence to the document. I believed that it came from the core of my father's personality, not a role or persona.

I've never been certain why he granted control of his legacy to me. I suspect he wanted someone to know of his prodigious output, the wide-ranging velocity of his mind. At the time he wrote the secret will, we had been at odds for over a decade. It bothered both of us, and we didn't know how to overcome the distance, blaming each other, ensuring hostility through the steady maintenance of old wounds. Attack and counterattack, intimidate and ignore. We raised the art of veiled criticism to its finest sophistication and talked against the other within the family.

Because my father made it abundantly clear that he might die at any moment, I kept the secret will for twenty-eight years, through many moves about the country. Each new location meant discarding clothes, books, and furniture, but I always knew where the secret will was stored. I wrapped it in plastic for protection. Dad never mentioned the will, and I didn't bring up the subject. His trust lay between us, unspoken and vital. When he died, it was the first item I packed before heading to Kentucky. As it turned out, I didn't need it—my siblings still weren't interested. I'd kept it safe for nothing. Nobody but me ever read the pages. No one cared but Dad.

On the long drive to Kentucky after his death, I watched for the Pottsville Escarpment, a geologic formation that indicated the edge of the Appalachians. Earlier I'd passed through Lexington, site of my birth, and wondered how my life might be if we'd stayed there, near my mother's family. What if I'd gone away to college instead of attending the closest one? What if I'd married one of my first four girlfriends? What if I'd stuck with my dream of being an actor? What if I hadn't hurt my knee so severely at age nineteen that I was forced back home in a plaster cast after leaving the hills forever, a pattern of departure and return that repeated many times until I realized the landscape would always hold me tight, that I could never escape, that in fact what I loved and felt most loyal to were the wooded hills, and not my father.

Chapter Five

MY FATHER'S full name was Andrew Jefferson Offutt V. As a child, he saw his name on three tombstones in a cemetery, a chilling sight that instilled a lifelong fear of joining them. This resulted in his decision to be cremated. Before I got home, his body was hauled out of the county for official incineration. The cremators cut open his chest to remove his heart implant. They placed the body in a cardboard box and slid it into a crematory that generated a fire of fifteen hundred degrees. Two hours of searing heat vaporized all organic matter, leaving pulverized bone, salt, and stray minerals.

Dad was an avowed agnostic, repeatedly emphasizing that he was not an atheist. In his opinion, disbelief created a religion of its own. This made for a brief conference with the director of memorial services. My sister and I rejected most options, including an urn or wooden box for Dad's ashes. We went home to choose appropriate music and an array of photographs that would slowly fade into one another on a TV during the service.

Three days after Dad died, the family convened at the house. The first action each of us took, unplanned and spontaneous, was

23

to slam the back door and stomp around the house—activities forbidden to us, reserved only for Dad. Then we laughed like maniacs, four middle-aged adults at last allowed to behave like children in our own home. My siblings stayed twelve miles away at a motel by the interstate. This was traditional—none of us slept in the house when we visited. The extra expense was worth the emotional safety. Dad never made us feel welcome and didn't care for the presence of grandchildren. He treated them the same way he'd treated us as kids—bullying and critical, angry at the breaking of his ever-changing rules about sound, laughter, and talking. An essential difference was that we knew the risks, but our children didn't.

The last time I took my young sons to Kentucky had ended badly. Dad began his standard browbeating of seven-year-old Sam, who'd left the bathroom door open. I was unable to respond, a failure that chafes me still. Instead of seeing my son as the target, I saw myself as a child—vulnerable and powerless—and it triggered such intense pain that I simply shut down. I lapsed into immobile silence as if frozen in place, my body separate from my mind, my emotions absent. I knew I should intervene on my son's behalf, but the child part of me was still terrified of my father's rage.

Rita, my wife at the time, had no such inner darkness. She came to me and said: "We have to go." Within fifteen minutes we packed our suitcases, made our stiff farewells, and drove to town. We didn't return to Kentucky for several years, a decision that was very painful for my mother. She'd saved all our toys for the grandchildren to play with on future visits—LEGOs, blocks, dollhouses, soldiers, and more than twenty board games. Three times she asked me to send my boys to her home by themselves. I refused without telling her the reason: I didn't want them to endure their grandfather's emotional abuse.

In my twenties and thirties, I called home often. Mom always answered and, after a brief conversation, put my father on the line. For a long time I thought she didn't like speaking to me. Later I learned that if she talked too long, Dad would get mad. When they added an extension for the second floor, Dad eavesdropped until he voiced a disagreement. At times they began their own conversation. I would listen, imagining them in different rooms of the house, talking on the phone. Now I was eavesdropping. Twice I gently hung up the phone, wondering how long they'd continue until noticing I wasn't there.

Over the years I came to dread three days per year that necessitated phone calls to my folks: Christmas, Dad's birthday, and Father's Day. A gnawing anxiety began two or three weeks before each holiday. I thought about the problem from various angles, foremost when to actually dial the number. As with everything in Dad's life, there were staunch rules regarding the phone. No calls in the morning or afternoon or during meals. Calling between five o'clock and six o'clock was acceptable, except Dad usually hadn't had a drink yet, which meant he'd be impatient, prone to anger. Six to seven was out due to supper. Calling between seven and eight was optimal—unless the Reds were on TV. Later was no good, because after a few drinks Dad rattled on nonstop, his slurred speech veering into the maudlin, his mood volatile.

I latched on to the idea of calling promptly at seven o'clock on the three days per year when I felt obligated to communicate with my father. Unfortunately, the line was often busy because my siblings had deduced the same ideal time. Despite Dad's claim of disliking the phone, he was a lonely man who enjoyed talking. If I said I needed to go, he'd simply launch into a new subject and orate for several minutes. We didn't really converse; I listened. Dad often threw verbal bait into the water—usually an opinion he knew I didn't share—seeking a disagreement, which for many years I snatched like a starving fish, eager for conversation even if it was a debate that ended in anger. Over time, I learned to recognize and ignore those traps. After a brief pause, he'd begin a monologue on a new subject. Never did he inquire about my wife, my sons, or me.

The only way I could get through these telephone calls was by having a drink first, then replenishing as Dad talked. Afterward, instead of merely feeling bad, I'd be drunk and feeling bad. I tried a new tactic—right after Dad answered, I informed him that I had to be somewhere in twenty minutes, but I wanted to call since it was Father's Day. I successfully employed this strategy for fifteen years.

When my work started getting published, Dad told me how he dealt with editors, a group of people he loathed. He'd make a list of subjects he wanted to address, then anticipate an editor's reactions and generate his own written responses. This way, no matter what an editor said on the phone, Dad was prepared and could not be taken by surprise. He applied the same pattern to family calls, building a scene in his head and behaving within his self-assigned role. The drawback came when family members lacked insight into his pre-scripted conversations. If someone didn't respond the way he'd imagined, Dad's frustration could easily escalate into anger.

One Christmas Dad sent me a hundred-dollar bill. It was the second time he'd ever given me cash, the first being forty bucks when I left home. A hundred dollars was a pleasant surprise. Previous Christmas gifts had included his discarded undershirts with stains in the armpits.

Reluctantly, I made the holiday phone call. Dad answered. By this time his phone had caller ID. He answered gruffly, without preamble or greeting. "Why'd you call, Chris?" he said.

"Uh, because it's Christmas."

"I know what day it is. I mean why did you call me?"

"To say 'Merry Christmas.'"

A long silence. I had no idea how to proceed.

"Are you there?" he said.

"Yes."

"Don't you have anything to say to me?"

"Sure, Dad. Merry Christmas. Hope it's a good one."

"You're not letting me say what I want to say."

Another long silence, which I broke. "I don't know what you want to say, Dad. But I'm listening."

"No, you're talking. Saying you're listening is talking."

"Well, that's why I called, just to talk."

The conversation descended into a tense silence. Dad finally told me that he'd planned his response to my thanking him for the money he'd sent. But I must have known that, since I was deliberately thwarting him.

"Thanks for the money," I said.

"What money?"

I didn't speak, unsure what my side of the pre-scripted conversation was supposed to be.

He spoke into the silence. "I said, 'What money?,' Chris."

"The hundred dollars. I appreciate it."

"What hundred dollars? Did I send you money?" He started laughing.

"Dad, is that what you wanted to say?"

"Yes."

"Okay," I said. "I have to go now."

Later, Mom called to talk with my sons, then put Dad on the phone. James was in middle school. During the conversation he lowered his voice and began giving me quick furtive glances. Afterward he told me that his grandfather had talked to him about Internet pornography, saying that porn fueled all technology and that James was lucky it was available to him online. I told James that scientific research fueled technology, not porn.

For the memorial service, Mom chose Friday afternoon at a local funeral home. Since the family hadn't paid for a fancy container, a table held an empty wooden box that represented his ashes. The box contained nothing, a fitting metaphor for a man who didn't allow himself to be known. No one from his family attended the service.

Dad had little tact and no sense of diplomacy but could engage anyone in conversation. Everyone in the county had Andy Offutt anecdotes. One often-repeated story concerned a man who'd lost an arm in an accident and kept his folded sleeve pinned in place. The precise circumstances changed with each telling, but the gist was that at a social gathering, in a voice loud enough for all to hear, my father threatened to "come over there and tear your other arm off," then laughed uproariously.

The sympathetic comments of the memorial attendees reflected brief encounters from decades back.

"You didn't meet a man like him every day."

"He was a character."

"God broke the mold when He made Andy."

"Put four kids through college and never left the house."

"He was a character."

"Your dad would say the most outrageous things."

"He was nice to me once."

"Andy didn't get along with many people, but I always liked him."

"He was a character."

"He was a character."

"He was a character."

The visitors drifted away. True to her Irish heritage, my mother pored over the guest book to learn who hadn't come, prepared to feel slighted. After everyone left, the ashes were presented to Mom, who gave them to me. The plastic container had the style of a large recipe box with a flip-top lid. Inside was a plastic bag filled with surprisingly heavy powder, tied off with a wire. Because I was driving, I tasked my son with transport. He snugged the box against his stomach, strapped safely beneath the seat belt. With my mother in the passenger seat, I drove slowly to avoid a wreck. One slip of the hand could drench us in the physical residue of Dad.

My father's only direct instructions regarding his death had been to open a bottle of hundred-proof bourbon with his name emblazoned on the label, and drink a toast. The quart of whiskey had sat on a high shelf for many years, a Christmas gift from my mother. I'd always considered it odd that Dad would place the bottle in full view of his chair, where a quick glance would remind him of his mortality. As I drove up the hill, it occurred to me that maybe I had it backward—maybe the bourbon watched over my father.

In the living room, Mom opened the special bottle and poured shots. We stood in a ragged circle, looking at one another. No one knew what to say, and I realized everyone was waiting for me. I lifted my glass. "To Andrew Offutt, father, husband, writer."

I placed the ashes on a shelf that held Dad's books published under his own name. In the next few days, we each added items to make a small shrine—photos, knives, a mug, a plaque, a Kentucky Derby hat. Everyone knew Dad wanted to be cremated, and we all assumed that someone else had information regarding the disposal of the ashes. As it turned out, he hadn't specified his intentions with anyone. Never a sentimental man, my father had no special spot in the woods, favorite view of the land, or relationship with a body of water. We didn't have an urn for a columbarium. Various options arose, but none took hold: saving the ashes to bury with Mom, dividing them among the survivors, or placing them in a rocket bound for outer space. After a while the subject trickled away and was abandoned. We were all putting off the decision, perhaps an effort to avoid a mistake that would have made Dad mad.

My siblings returned to their respective homes. My wife and I stayed the next three months in Kentucky to help with legal issues and Mom's future plans. As a child, I never knew what my mother thought or felt. She didn't talk much. My primary memory consisted of her moving quietly about the house carrying objects from room to room. She carried out tasks with focused intent and followed strict routines: shopping one day, cleaning another, laundry on a third. The rest of the time she typed.

Mom was a cipher to me then and, to some extent, still is. Her standard response to any inquiry was a variation of "I'm fine" or "Everything's great" or "I have no regrets." If asked her preference about anything—an outing, a meal, a drink—she invariably reversed the question to "What do you want?" Her opinions were reflective of Dad's, a kind of psychic mirror. She avoided conflict by keeping her feelings to herself, and the result was marital accord.

A week after the memorial service, I took Mom to a greenhouse built of plastic sheeting. Mom selected a plant with white flowers, then smiled, shook her head, and chose red flowers instead.

"Your father was color-blind," she said. "I only bought white flowers so he could see them."

She took the red ones home. After fifty years Mom planted flowers she liked in her own backyard.

Chapter Six

THE LOSS of a parent takes away a kind of umbrella against the inclement weather of life. Regardless of condition—tattered fabric and broken spokes—it had always been at hand, offering the potential of protection and safety. Dad's death made me the nominal head of the family, maker of decisions, next in line to die. Now I had to provide my own umbrella—for myself, my siblings, and my mother.

Mom decided to sell the house and move to Mississippi. My wife and I began clearing her house, filled with the accumulation of five decades. Furniture stood against the wall of every room, often piled with objects—pillows, books, magazines. Each closet was stuffed floor-to-ceiling. Depression-raised, my parents threw nothing away—the basement contained junk culled from the rest, the discards of the discards.

I began with Dad's clothes—forty pairs of fleece sweatpants and pullovers, and sixty silk shirts, all bought by mail. One pair of pants had a large lump in a pocket. I checked for cash but found an unused tissue, which meant the pants hadn't been washed since he wore them. The last hand inside the pocket had been his. I underwent a deep sorrow but quickly locked my feelings away, exactly as my father always had. Emotions would interfere with the tasks at hand, slow my progress, render me weak and vulnerable.

I worked twelve hours a day. We made daily trips to town: donating books to the library; clothes and household items to Christian Social Services; furniture to the university theater department. On the way home, we stopped at the liquor store to get more boxes. The strongest ones were designed to hold bourbon, the poison that had killed Dad.

For several years my father lived in a large La-Z-Boy chair, upholstered in leather, the right arm burnished smooth from moving the TV remote control. The seat was lodged in a permanent tilt to accommodate the favor he gave his bad leg, subject of a mysterious malady never diagnosed: nerves, arthritis, bone, something. Doctors could not discover the ailment. It bothered Dad for many years, leaving him unable to fly in an airplane, his reason for not visiting his adult children. He told me it was a "ghost wound," scar tissue below the surface where he'd been stabbed while serving Genghis Khan. He regarded the pain as evidence of reincarnation. He stressed that Khan's army was cavalry-based and he'd been a lowly foot soldier, nothing fancy. Dad reveled in the essential humility of this role.

Mom didn't want to keep his chair but felt uncomfortable donating it to Social Services. I called my childhood friend Faron, at one time nicknamed "Hollywood" for his handsome looks. He'd known my father for fifty years. Faron was a Henderson, a name in good stead in the county, unsullied by scandal or sin. He had three brothers, including Sonny, who had drained the basement in winter. One brother joined the navy and left the hills for good. The rest remained. As each aged, he came to resemble his father more, and I wondered if it was the same for me.

Faron and his wife arrived to help us pack. Faron had been a logger, a telephone lineman, and a carpenter. He broke horses and rode a motorcycle. He now worked as a car detailer. His hair was cut in a "Kentucky Waterfall," a long mullet that reached midchest when combed forward. I asked him what he called his hairstyle, and after hesitating, he looked me in the eye and said: "Outdated." We laughed as we always had, our dead fathers momentarily forgotten. Faron and I carried Dad's chair to his truck. He was laughing as he accelerated up the grade and around the curve, his hair streaming from the window.

I gathered Dad's guns and went through them. A revolver was broken, the crane snapped off the cylinder, not worth repairing. Two were rusted to ruin. I took a shotgun and a rifle to visit Faron's brother, a master gunsmith who won awards for marksmanship with muzzle-loading rifles he built by hand. Randy sat in his garage surrounded by tools, gun parts, a motorcycle, and chunks of gorgeous wood. He greeted me as if he'd seen me last week instead of a decade back. We could have been kin—bearded and bespectacled, with sandy-gray hair and potbellies.

Randy cleaned Dad's guns while we talked. The Remington single-shot was made in 1936, the stock a rich tiger walnut, the action smooth, the sights still true. My grandfather used it to hunt small game during the Depression, then gave it to Dad. We walked to Randy's gun range and ran several rounds through the rifle. He was impressed by my ability to hit a beer can at twenty-five yards. I shrugged it off, secretly pleased, and gave credit to the rifle. "Good gun," Randy said. "Come see me." I nodded and drove away, grateful to know him, to know all the Hendersons.

For a long time I believed I'd had two childhoods—one in the house, and another outside—running parallel, drastically different. Years later I realized I'd had four distinct childhoods, indoors and out, plus a division of "before Dad worked at home" and the abrupt transition to his constant presence in the house.

My brother and I shared a bedroom on the second floor. Inside a clothes closet was another door that opened to a narrow staircase leading to the dark attic. I was absolutely convinced that ghosts lived up there. The exterior wall of the house held a set of closed, decorative shutters. They were fastened to the brick on the other side of the wall at the foot of the steps. I believed that after I went to sleep, ghosts descended the steps from the attic and used the shutters to leave the house and kill people, returning before I woke up. Eventually they would enter the house through the mysterious closet and kill the family. It was my job to protect my brother and sisters.

Before going to sleep, I arranged rocks beneath my blanket in specific patterns designed to keep the ghosts at bay. I developed the habit of sleepwalking, leaving the room to awaken elsewhere, occasionally outside. A few times I came to consciousness sitting in the bathroom, my mother pressing a damp cloth to my forehead, urging me to wake up. She later told me the whole thing perplexed her, but since I always awakened, she didn't worry about it. I never told her about the ghosts and she never asked about the rocks in my bed.

Dad needed a home office, and my sisters' bedroom was the best option. They would take my bedroom, with a new wall added for privacy. The attic would be renovated for my brother and me. Before the carpenters arrived, I decided to explore the attic during the day. I opened the closet door and stood at the bottom of the stairs, staring into the darkness above. I put one foot on the bottom step and immediately pulled it back. The next day I was able to keep my foot in place longer, and the day after that I momentarily stood on the bottom step. In this fashion, over a period of days, I crept up the steps until I was crouching at the top. As fast as possible, I jumped into the attic and pulled the string to a bare bulb hanging from the ceiling. The attic consisted of exposed beams, studs, and rafters. Without insulation or ventilation, the room was extremely hot. Wasps droned overhead.

Sitting on the floor was a cardboard box containing paperbacks with plain yellow covers. I plucked one at random and opened it. I knew right away that I shouldn't be reading it, but I didn't want to stop because it gave me a warm tingling inside my body. My stomach tightened and my lips became dry. I crouched over the box for an hour. There were about twenty of these books. I quickly learned to skim for the good parts, which were either graphic sex using language I'd never seen, or detailed accounts of spanking women with big backsides.

My brother called me for supper and I arranged the books in the order I'd found them and went downstairs. After years of being scared of the attic, I now wanted to rush back upstairs. For a week I secretly read hard-core pornography until my mother cleared the area for the carpenters. I was eleven years old.

That same summer a dentist pulled four of my permanent molars to create sufficient space to move the rest of my teeth around my mouth. I wore a full set of braces for two years—upper and lower—the only ones in the county. Every morning I replaced four rubber bands that crisscrossed between my jaws. At night I slept wearing a metal bit that locked into my teeth and buckled behind my head. My mouth ached most of the time. I'd always been a rough-and-tumble kid, and the inside of my lips bled from ragged wounds sustained by rural life. I learned to ignore throbbing gums, cut lips, and the spitting of blood. Pain relegated itself to a distant nagging, similar to the itch of an insect bite.

The carpenters worked all summer, and in August my brother and I moved to our new room in the attic. Each night we stepped into the dim closet at the foot of the steps. Our room above was completely dark, and the light switch was at the top of the stairs. I inhaled deeply and held my breath. I placed my hands on the doorjamb and catapulted myself up the steps, knowing just where to place my feet to avoid each creak. At the top of the stairs, my open palm hit the light switch, and I jerked my head to check for ghosts. They were always gone, having managed to flee moments before my sudden arrival. It was then safe enough for my brother to climb the steps.

Decades later he told me he'd been grateful that I went upstairs first. Every time he ascended the steps as an adult, something cold always passed through his body. Later, I asked my younger sister if there was any part of the house she was afraid of. She was silent for a moment, then shook her head and said, "I was afraid of the whole house."

Over the past thirty-five years, our attic bedroom had shifted in the traditional way of an abandoned nest—first to a sewing room, then a study when my mother attended college, and now a storage chamber for junk. Narrow paths flanked tall stacks of goods that included Christmas decorations from the fifties, clothes from the sixties, and high school yearbooks from the seventies. The roof leaked. There was a vague smell of mildew, rot, and squirrel urine. My bed was an odd-sized piece of foam rubber that was crumbling and gnawed by mice. Beneath it lay remnants from childhood: a few paperback books, an empty wallet, a pile of seventh-grade love letters, a cigar box filled with wheat pennies, three diaries, and a dead bat.

I found a framed charcoal sketch of my brother that someone drew when we were kids. I stared at the drawing for a long time. It looked more like my brother now than it did then, as if the artist understood that a portrait is future memory made tangible. I wandered among the maze of piled objects, touching this and that. It was like being at a yard sale, going through the remains of another person's life. No one occupied this space anymore, living or dead. I had become my own ghost, haunting my past.

I went outside and used a ladder to climb onto the narrow porch roof. The closed shutters were screwed permanently into the brick. No secret door existed. There was just a man standing alone on a roof, facing a wall.

Chapter Seven

FOR MOST people, childhood is a refuge of simpler times. The increasing responsibilities of adulthood imbue the past with innocence and joy—a seemingly endless summer, the vastness of a night sky, winter's fade to the bouyancy of spring. Childhood improves as we age and get further away from it. Not so for my father. He rarely talked of his early years except in dark tones, with the occasional anecdote or an obliquely bitter reference. The story of his youth is vague, shrouded in pain and difficulty.

Dad was born in 1934, at the height of the Great Depression. The Offutt family owned a farm near Taylorsville, with a large main house and a log cabin for sharecroppers. To save the farm from repossession by the bank, my grandparents rented out the main house and moved into the cabin, where Dad spent his formative years. Only two artifacts survive from his life on the farm, the oldest being a certificate from the Louisville *Courier-Journal* proclaiming him the winner of the Spencer County Spelling Bee in 1944. The second is a 1946 photograph of Dad and his sister standing on rocky ground in summer. They wear overalls and straw hats. Visible in the background is their log home, the joints so heavily chinked with white cement that the structure appears to be horizontally striped. Dad faces the camera with an expression of dissatisfaction.

He returned to the farm once, forty years later, asking me to accompany him. Dad drove very fast, his wrists crossed at the top of the steering wheel, severely limiting his ability to maneuver the car. I tilted my seat back and breathed slowly for the first half hour before offering to drive. That way, I said, you can navigate and look around at the old familiar turf. As a former salesman, Dad was a malleable mark—he admired the calm logic of persuasion. I drove the rest of the way and he talked nonstop, a recounting of memory soaked in sorrow.

The log house was hot in summer and cold in winter. Dad was shy as a kid, sensitive and withdrawn, a bookworm and mama's boy with no interest in sports. He despised the tedious labor of dairy farming. Dad didn't like his father, who, in his early forties, began wearing shirts of a floral design and going to town at odd hours. A large bouquet of roses arrived anonymously at his funeral. When Dad told me this, I assumed my grandfather had a girlfriend in town. But Dad concluded that his father was a latent homosexual and the roses had come from a man. I nodded, thinking that Dad's need to eliminate his father's influence was so great that he chose the worst-case scenario for rural men of his generation. Nevertheless, Dad had two positive memories.

At age ten, he joined his father and a neighbor on a hunting venture, armed with a .22-caliber rifle. A scared rabbit began its unpredictable hopping flight. Dad snapped off a shot and killed it with an incredibly lucky bullet. His father was inordinately proud of him—less for having hit the rabbit and more for having done so in front of his neighbor. Dad never hunted again, preferring to end as he began, with utter perfection. The only other positive interaction occurred during the depths of a brutally cold winter. My grandfather took Dad outside to urinate against the barn wall with him, side by side. The twin streams slowed to slush as they ran down the oak boards, freezing to ice before reaching the ground.

After leaving the farm, Dad attended the University of Louisville on an academic scholarship from the Ford Foundation. The plan was for smart people from disadvantaged circumstances to skip their senior year in high school and enroll in college. Dad suited all the requirements and had just won a Kentucky-wide fiction-writing contest for a short story called "The Devil's Soul."

During Dad's sophomore year, his father died suddenly at age forty-five. His mother sold the car and found work at a bank. Dad responded by embracing college life and constructing a new identity. He took up smoking, drinking, and playing cards. He became president of his fraternity. For two years he was in the Air Force Reserve Officer Training Corps, hoping to be a pilot, until his color-blindness prevented him from flying. He was editor and cartoonist for *Static,* the AFROTC campus periodical, and editor for *The Cardinal,* the student newspaper. In his senior year Dad won a national science fiction contest sponsored by *If* magazine, his first professional publication.

On the way to Taylorsville, Dad and I got lost several times on dirt roads that petered out to walls of forest. Late in the day, at the end of a freshly paved road, we discovered the farm's main house. Past that was the log cabin. I parked and we approached on foot. The walls were fully intact, the corners still notched tightly together after 150 years. The windows were gone and poison oak covered the front. The roof was caved in. The floor had rotted away and trees grew within, their branches swaying above the walls. My father stared silently for a long time at the ruin. He didn't move. I understood that he was looking at the cabin but seeing something else.

I left him alone and wandered the land, trying to imagine his early years. The terrain of western Kentucky is very different from the hills in the east. Spencer County is part of the Salt River Basin, a rolling landscape with a vast expanse of sky and wind rustling the hay fields. On all sides the land slowly rose to meet the horizon as if the farm sat inside a wide and shallow bowl. I could see why he left and never returned. He'd grown up in a crater.

The land surrounding the cabin was too overgrown to enter, the yard a tangle of brush and weeds. We walked to the old barn, which was in better shape, having been maintained for use. Six feet tall with long legs, Dad always walked at a fast pace. Now he moved slowly, as if in a fugue state, somnolent but highly alert, taking in everything. He stared at the hayloft for a long time and finally spoke: "I made my sister jump out of there once. Dad didn't like it. Made me kneel on rocks all day."

He walked the length of the barn, peering into each stall, then stepped outside. I followed him. He unzipped his pants. We stood side by side and urinated against the old oak boards, then got in the car and left. We made the drive home without talking, the longest period I ever saw him silent. He never mentioned the trip again.

The deprivation and indignity of growing up during the Depression imprinted my father with intense frugality. Dad salvaged narrow slivers of soap, the grimy remains of bars that he rescued before the water rinsed them down the sink. He dampened each piece and formed a new chunk of soap, lined with dirt and hair. He placed it by the sink, where it lay untouched, hardening as it dried, cracking into dark fissures.

My father didn't trust banks and disliked large government. After his death I found small bundles of cash tucked away in various areas of the house, and enough canned food, liquor, and ammunition to survive a prolonged siege. In the early years of writing, he was often broke or nearly so and had legal trouble with the IRS. My aunt and grandmother had set up a college fund for my siblings and me, but Dad took the money for himself. He sold my comic book collection of fifteen hundred titles and kept the proceeds. My brother changed his mailing address after Dad cashed his college financial aid check.

My siblings and I grew up with the specter of the Depression and our father's belief in its return. For our future benefit, he stock-piled gold, silver, and jewels. Each time I visited home, Dad took me aside to deliver private information about his hiding places, always with an attitude of utmost secrecy and the implication that he was telling me and only me. *When the time comes*, he said, his voice lowered for dramatic effect, *and it will.* He told me to search the furnace vents. He pointed to the top of a custom-designed bookshelf in his office, the molding of which concealed three secret compartments. *Up there*, he said. *Gold for the family.* I felt honored by his confidential tone, his trust.

Questions were seldom a good idea with Dad, as he tended to interpret them as criticism. Peace was maintained by agreeable nods and his preferred response of "Yes, sir." As a result, I never asked which particular heating ducts held the bounty. Neither did my siblings, who'd also been repeatedly informed of secret caches about the house. He told each of us that he'd stored semi-precious stones outside the back door, strewn among a "rock garden" consisting of gravel and creek rock. It was a miniature shrine to a crumbling statue of Thulsa Doom, a powerful necromancer in the fictional world of Conan the Barbarian. Dad wrote nine novels set in Robert E. Howard's imaginary Hyborian Age, using the profits to enclose a side porch. Etched into the cement floor was "Crom," the name of Conan's personal god. In a very real sense, the new room represented the booty of Conan, while the valuable gems in the yard turned out to be worthless rocks polished smooth in a geologist's tumbler.

Many years ago a friend of mine from a wealthy family in New England told me that, upon hearing of an elder's death, the survivors rushed to the bank to clean out the safe-deposit box. Cash, jewelry, and bearer bonds were up for grabs. After Dad died, my brother and I undertook our quest for plunder as a team to avoid the appearance of "rushing to the floor vents."

We began with those nearest to Dad's chair and expanded concentrically, room by room. The metal vent covers rested in slots above the ductwork, which ran like veins throughout the house. I got on my hands and knees and inserted a mirror into the openings while my brother bounced the beam of a flashlight along the horizontal passages. We found plastic soldiers, Tinker Toys, Barbie shoes, spiderwebs, mouse droppings, and finally a canvas bag layered with dust. We lifted it onto the floor and crouched before it. Inside was a velvet fabric wrapped around objects with very little weight. We slowly unfolded the cloth, rapt and solemn in the face of our father's fabled treasure: a soup ladle, a salad fork, and two very small cups, all made of sterling silver.

My brother left, and a few days later my sister arrived to help. We embarked upon the difficult task of investigating the secret compartments in the bookshelves of Dad's office. The windows had been shut for twenty years, and Dad hadn't occupied the room in ten. Summer's heavy heat had me sweating through my clothes, while the dust affected my sister's asthma. Even the planning stage proved arduous. The three panels were located at the very top of the wall-to-wall bookcase, pressed against the high ceiling. I couldn't reach them by standing on a chair. We moved stacks of porn to make space for a rickety wooden stepladder. My sister held it while I ascended. The middle panel was a long narrow trapdoor that had to be opened first, in order to allow access to the two flanking compartments. The entire bookcase had listed hard toward the corner, pinching the humidity-swollen wood. The middle panel wouldn't open.

My sister handed me a hammer and screwdriver. Two light taps snapped the panel open to reveal a narrow compartment, just high enough to be out of my range of vision. I gingerly stood on the top step, which was split along the grain. I glanced at my sister to make sure she was holding the ladder. Her earnest expression sparked a flash of memory—I recalled standing on a wooden box placed on a chair while she handed me a new lightbulb for a ceiling fixture in her bedroom. Our parents had been out of town. We'd been on our own, same as now.

Using a flashlight, I peered at a massive mouse nest in the secret compartment. Beyond that were fifteen plastic pill bottles, which I removed. The ladder swayed as if windblown. Working together the same way we'd changed the lightbulb as children, we inspected the other two compartments. After gathering everything in a box, we carried it downstairs and laid out the final artifacts of our legendary inheritance.

SILVER

14 Liberty dollars
1 Kennedy half-dollar
1 Franklin half-dollar
2 Washington quarters
34 Mercury dimes
48 Roosevelt dimes

JEWELS

Black star of India
Garnet
Opal
Tigereye

Amethyst
Moonstone
Rutilated quartz (*fleche d'amour*)
Tourmalated quartz (Cupid dart)

GOLD

One Cross pen, tarnished and inoperable
One bird's nest containing four robin eggs sprayed with
    gold paint

My sister was disappointed in our father's treasure, citing its worthlessness as evidence of his distorted view of the world. Dad had filled us with his own delusions, which we dutifully believed, in the hope that items of genuine value might surface. Instead, we were heirs to hidden junk.

I carefully sorted the goods, trying to understand why he might have considered them worthy of preservation. The coins were old silver, remarkable for the bell-like peal they emitted when bounced off wood. Unfortunately, all were worn smooth from excessive handling. Despite their secure location and long-term storage capped in plastic tubes, they had no value beyond a coin dealer's woeful term of "melt value."

In the 1980s, Dad purchased many packets of semi-precious stones through the mail. Each came with an official Certificate of Authenticity signed by a representative of the International Gem Finders. The flimsy papers crumbled as I unfolded them to read:

This document certifies that the enclosed acquisition content has been professionally evaluated by our supplier and guaranteed authentic.

I admired the vagueness of the language as a marketing tool. "Enclosed acquisition content" could refer to any item whatsoever, thereby allowing the certificate to be slipped into a variety of packages. My father patronized two companies: North American Minerals and Gem Collectors International. Both were owned by Raffoler, a company bombarded by lawsuits for deceptive advertising, selling shoddy merchandise, misrepresenting products, running illegal lotteries disguised as sweepstakes, and violating mail order rules for timely shipment. The gemstones Dad so carefully hoarded had the same low value they'd had at the time of purchase, which is to say a few dollars.

My father loved ordering goods through the mail, which he began in childhood with Sears, Roebuck. He continued this practice during the 1950s and '60s with his purchases of porn advertised in the classified pages of men's magazines; in the 1970s with Frederick's of Hollywood and Lew Magram; then videos in the '80s and DVDs during the '90s. In his final years he ordered tens of thousands of vitamins guaranteed to keep him alive longer than medically possible—which apparently worked.

Anyone who has ever purchased goods through the mail understands the daily tension that builds as the hour nears for the mail to arrive. Finally the long-awaited parcel arrives. The true connoisseur—as my father was—doesn't tear into it immediately, but sets it aside to be savored after the rest of the mail has been opened. Then the package can be examined by weight and size, shaken slightly side to side, head cocked to listen for evidence of the tantalizing contents. Next is a penknife's precise slit along the edge, allowing only the tip of the blade entry to prevent accidental cutting of the cargo. Last comes the slow withdrawal of a shirt, a book, a packet of gemstones, a triple-X videotape, a pair of slippers, a time-saving gadget, pamphlets of privately printed porn, a solar-powered calculator, a flashlight that never needs batteries, a German porn magazine, a complex hand tool that replaces every item you own, a cup that won't tip over, a pack of fetish photographs, a lightbulb that will never burn out, French porn, a clock that keeps perfect time, a selection of porn paperbacks, a swatch of cloth that cleans anything but never needs cleaning itself, bondage comic books, a knife that always stays sharp, vintage nude pinups, rechargeable batteries, porn from Italy, a magnifying glass that reacts to individual eyesight, dozens of items guaranteed to be unbreakable or your money back. Countless such gadgets filled every closet and drawer in the house.

The golden bird's nest with four eggs embarrassed my mother. She'd spray-painted it many years ago and was immediately admonished by Dad for doing so. Mom believed its presence in the hidden compartment was intended as a posthumous reprimand directed at her. Her guilt saddened me. I wanted to protect her from her own emotions.

I told her that, as a kid on the farm, Dad had placed fake eggs in poultry roosts, hoping to induce hens to lay more eggs. This farming custom gave rise to the term "nest egg" as a sum of money earmarked for future use. Maybe Dad intended the nest and four eggs as motivation for his kids to go off and earn their own money. This satisfied my mother, but ultimately I discarded the premise.

My father's sense of humor was influenced by fraternity parties in the fifties and Johnny Carson in the sixties—clever, naughty, and knowing—aimed at the middle ground, distinctly sophomoric. He liked being the fellow who'd make an inappropriate comment for the sake of a laugh. Dad enjoyed visual pranks such as a rubber snake nestled in a windowsill, toy soldiers in the Christmas crèche, or a fake birthday gift consisting of an empty box. I believe the bird's nest was intended as a joke, carefully hidden before his health prevented him from climbing the steps. I imagined him chuckling as he stood on a chair, his long arms easily reaching the trapdoor overhead. He tucked the nest in the tiny cubbyhole, enjoying the thought of us finding a genuine golden nest and four eggs. I loved him for the diabolic arranging of a prank he'd never see to fruition. Every time I think of the nest, I grin. *Up there, gold for the family.*

Chapter Eight

THROUGHOUT THE summer I felt bad for compelling my mother to participate in the steady dismantling of her home, and I sought small ways to make her happy. She read mystery novels at a fierce pace and kept them in stacks on the floor of various rooms. After clearing the living room of my father's books, I displayed Mom's collection on the shelves. She admired them daily, saying, "My books. You put my books up." Her joy moved me, as I understood that the house was at last becoming hers.

During meals I did what I'd always done—entertain Mom with jokes. She was a good audience, a skill developed from decades of living with a man who liked to talk. After I left home, it was hard for me to trust information I received from Mom. Due to the difficulties between my father and me, she always tried to present Dad in the best light—on the phone, in person, and by letter. After he died, she quit.

I took a break from clearing the house to finish a TV pilot for a network. The deadline was approaching. I set my laptop on Dad's desk. Writing there felt strange, but I had little choice. Given the general disarray of the house, his office was the only private room. Over the years, I'd written in hotels, rooming houses, cars, a basement, a garage, and a shed. Once I began, the location no longer mattered. I lost track of time, forgot to eat or drink. The imaginary world became real enough that it didn't feel like writing but more like observing actual people and transcribing their words and actions.

While working on the screenplay, I occasionally stopped to raise my head from the computer. Only then did the realization of my whereabouts crash into me. I saw the same images my father had when he paused in his work: a poster for the movie *Barbarian Queen,* depicting five women armed with swords, dressed like strippers. Above his desk hung a laminated Sunday cartoon of Snoopy with a typewriter and the caption "Good writing is hard work." Another wall held Samuel Johnson's famous line: "No man but a blockhead ever wrote except for money." Like my father, I was trying to live up to both Snoopy and Johnson.

The brick walls insulated external sound but kept noise in the house, and I began to understand Dad's resentment of interruption. I could hear my mother in the kitchen, my wife walking overhead. With four children and two dogs, the sound of cars at the foot of the hill, and the consistent echo of rural gunfire, my father had sat here and written hundreds of books. I should be able to finish a screenplay.

In a sense, my father died the moment I learned he was going to die. On the phone, it was like talking to a ghost. Now I began to wonder if he was there, overseeing my progress with his critical judgment. Though I often glanced about, I saw nothing. As a child I'd been afraid of his office, and now I was interacting with the imprint of my former fear. I saw things that weren't there. I heard voices that didn't exist. Part of me wanted to assign those nebulous sensations to something palpable and real. I ignored the impulse and completed the screenplay on time. Mom said it was what my father would have wanted.

At night I watched the Reds on TV with the volume down, listening to the play-by-play on the radio, as I'd done with Dad. I drank his whiskey and read his books. His library included numerous volumes on the supernatural, and at night I read about ghosts and anticipated my father's appearance. With a sudden clarity, I understood that Dad had haunted this house while he was alive, and I was haunting it now.

Each of my siblings privately urged me to destroy everything in his office. I understood their shared view. Porn had little appeal to any of us, and we all knew the office contained an enormous amount. An overt sexuality pervaded the house in the form of books not adequately concealed or art depicting nude women on the walls. It was embarrassing when guests visited. We all left home at age seventeen, having been taught secrecy, particularly about his career. As a result we rarely talked about Dad with other people. His death released us from the necessity of silence. Destroying his papers would be a means of retaliation, of destroying the silence itself. But I couldn't do it.

As a son, I wanted an opportunity to understand him further through his work. In the following weeks each of my siblings privately thanked me for taking on the job of the office. They expressed concern that I'd be overwhelmed by the effort or emotionally done in. I explained that with Dad dead, I was able to separate the writer from the man, and the man from our father. They only partially believed me. As it turned out, it was only partially true.

Chapter Nine

AS A child, I explored Dad's office the first time while my parents attended a party in town. I waited until my siblings were in bed. The fewer who knew of my secret activities, the better, a way of thinking I'd certainly inherited from Dad. Before entering, I used a ruler to measure the distance between the edge of the door and the jamb, writing the number of inches on my wrist, reasoning that if the space was too large or small, Dad would know and I'd face his wrath.

Those early attempts at discerning insight into my father were little more than spelunking an unknown cave. I moved in quietly, able to see only what was illuminated by flashlight, my fear increased by the darkness and shadows. I found a stack of *Playboy* magazines. A surprising item was an embroidered patch, the kind people sewed on a dungaree jacket. Encased in a small frame, it sat on a shelf so as to be visible to Dad at his typewriter. It said: "You're a fuckin' genius." The frame gave it an official quality. I thought it was an award from an unknown entity that recognized my father as a genius, and for many years I believed he was.

After his death, I began a more careful examination of his office. My general understanding was that Dad had occasionally written porn to supplement his income, a pattern followed by many writers. Now, I realized that wasn't the case. For half his life my father passed as a science fiction writer while actually functioning as a professional pornographer. Dad's first eleven books were porn. The extent of his output surprised me, since the secret will had implied a fraction of what I discovered.

Throughout his writing life, Dad remained staunchly emphatic that he himself did not use multiple pen names. His persona, John Cleve, had sixteen pseudonyms. John Cleve had his own wardrobe, stationery, and signature. Most important, my father liked *being* John Cleve. John Cleve wrote sex books, was a 1970s swinger, and had no kids. John Cleve was free.

By the time Dad died, he hadn't worked in his office in a decade. Before that it was seldom cleaned beyond an occasional vacuuming and a light dusting as high as my mother could reach, which wasn't far. A narrow path wound between precarious stacks of porn, an outmoded printer, a broken copy machine, and three computers. Dad steadfastly refused an online connection, saying he feared the government would be able to peek inside his computer and learn about his porn. I considered this evidence of his paranoia and lack of technological understanding. Two months after his death, the NSA admitted they'd spied on hundreds of thousands of U.S. citizens via the Internet.

My father was more hoarder than collector, and I began by throwing away the obvious junk: rusted pocketknives, corroded flashlights, broken office equipment, a hockey puck, empty bottles of expensive beer, and dozens of tin boxes that once held fancy Scotch. The office decor reminded me of a college fraternity house with its implied pride in drinking and manliness. There was nothing personal or sentimental. His possessions consisted of gifts from fans at science fiction conventions, books, manuscripts, and thousands of letters. I learned to operate in a very specific way: examine each item, evaluate its importance, keep it or throw it away. The pressure of constant decision was relentless. I'd grown up terrified of this room and now I was in charge of it, like an inmate becoming a warden. I felt as if I were trespassing.

As a kid, I'd left his office quickly, giving a swift and nervous glance at the closet, which was always shut. Never seeing its contents gave the closet enormous clout; it was Pandora's box with a doorknob. The wood casing had expanded from humidity and I had to jerk the door open. The loud sound alarmed me, as if Dad would hear it and I'd get in trouble. I glanced furtively about. Nothing was there but the dusty, smoke-smelling room. The closet contained a wall of deep shelves that were a wreck of papers, books, magazines, computer manuals, and manila envelopes containing manuscripts. Wadded into a musty ball was a John Cleve shirt, now mildewed and rotting. A trail of dried mouse droppings led to a large nest composed of tattered manuscript pages. Twined within the rodent's home was the shed skin of a snake. I jumped back and slammed the door shut.

Throughout my childhood, the most familiar adult refrain was: "Watch for snakes." Standard practice in the hills was to kill any snake without wasting time trying to figure out what it was. My seventh-grade teacher taught us that poisonous snakes had a vertical pupil, but getting close enough to see the eyes put you at risk. Everyone I knew feared snakes: tough men, brave boys, women who could slaughter livestock without qualm. After discovering the snakeskin in the closet, I went downstairs and drank a glass of water. No doubt the snake was a harmless constrictor that had traveled to the second floor, discovered the mouse nest, eaten its fill, rested, and sought the next meal. The snake was long gone, its shed skin the ghost of its passage.

I returned to Dad's office and stood alert as a bandit, sweating and nervous. It ran through my mind that a case could be made for an adult facing childhood fears, both metaphoric and real, but none of that claptrap really applied. I was genuinely afraid of snakes. Under my father's orders, I had to clear out the closet. I did so quickly.

Two tall columns of paperback porn occupied the top shelf. Mixed in was a copy of *A Sport and a Pastime*, by James Salter, published in 1967. The cover proclaimed it a celebrated new underground classic, a feast for the sexual gourmet, and compared the writing to that of Henry Miller, one of my father's early heroes. Dad's insurance agency calling card marked page fifty. I held the book gingerly, astounded by its discovery, stashed away for forty-five years.

James Salter had been a guest teacher at Iowa during my years as a graduate student. So many people wanted to work with him that he screened us, reading sample work first, followed by a personal meeting. He was over sixty, charming and urbane on the surface, with a fierce steeliness lurking below. My interview didn't go well. He demanded to know what I could learn from him, since my subject matter of Kentucky was unfathomably different from his— wealthy people on the East Coast. I became angry. Here was one more older man presenting himself as an obstacle. Outraged and irate, I told Salter that content didn't matter, people were people, and I wanted to study with him because I admired his prose. I cut our meeting short and left, convinced that Iowa was a mistake. I'd never be a writer, and I only wanted to be one because of my father. The next day Salter posted a class list, with my name being one of the lucky twelve.

Many young writers believe in the myth of mentorship, but

I'd never sought a role model. I'd known one writer in my life—Dad—and naively surmised they'd all be like him: controlling, pretentious, cruel, and overbearing. My attitude at Iowa was one of belligerence. Established writers were the enemy, and my job was to overthrow their stranglehold on the fortress of literature. Despite my resistance, Salter helped me learn to improve my work. He'd gone to college at West Point and behaved as if students were enlisted soldiers and he was an officer, one who'd roll up his sleeves and mingle with his young charges. We went hiking together, leaving the trail for the local woods I knew well. He was unflagging in his energy, both physical and mental. He remarked that seeing me in the woods was like watching me write stories.

I never saw my father in the woods. He didn't walk them and remained oddly incurious about the landscape he'd chosen. It was enough for him to be surrounded by the heavy forest. The seclusion of the house matched the solitude within him, the immense isolation of his mind and its constant, rapid machinations.

After filling fifty garbage bags from his office, I could not see any difference other than a haze of disturbed dust hanging in the air. The room seemed more cluttered, with no space for organizing and packing. My eyes stung and I was developing a cough. Essentially I'd redistributed the contents into new piles. Based on approximately three hundred feet of bookshelf, I anticipated two days to pack the books. The allotted time period doubled immediately, then tripled. Every shelf held another row of books directly behind it—all pornography. I found several bottles of bourbon and dozens of recent manuscripts by Turk Winter, the persona who'd replaced John Cleve as my father's primary persona in the mid-eighties.

For the next several days I ate little. I guzzled water and sweated through my clothes until they were stiff with salt. I moved in a somnolent daze. Twice I noticed my mother staring at me from the hall. She said she'd been startled, that I looked so much like Dad, she thought I was him. I hugged her silently and went back to work. Later she began referring to me as "John Cleve, Jr.," a sobriquet that made me uncomfortable.

The project felt less like clearing a room and more like prospecting within his mind. The top layer was disorganized and heavy with porn. As I sorted like an archaeologist backward through time, I saw a remarkable mind at work, the gradual shifting from intellectual interest in literature, history, and psychology to an obsession with the darker elements of sex.

For decades he subscribed to magazines and kept them in stacks: *Ramparts. Intellectual Digest. Psychology Today. New Times. Galaxy. If. Playboy. Omni. Geo. National Geographic. Smithsonian.* He studied robotics, genetics, medicine, physics, and war before gunpowder. Two dozen books covered the history of ancient Greece and Rome. Mixed throughout was pornography in every form: magazines, photographs, drawings, pamphlets, a deck of cards, cartoons, books of erotic art from antiquity to the twenty-first century, calendars, pinups, postcards, collections of naughty jokes. A pile of dusty catalogs from Frederick's of Hollywood ran back fifty years.

After a week I no longer considered the undertaking in terms of my father and me, or even as a writer going through another writer's papers. My thinking shifted to a more formal role, that of an archivist faced with an enormous holding of raw material. I organized and collated and distributed. I stopped looking at pictures or reading, and simply made decisions in my head—*this goes here, that goes over there, here's a new one for a fresh pile.* I could have been sorting marbles or Tupperware.

I packed everything in liquor boxes and taped them shut. The stacked cartons made a double-rowed wall that blocked four windows in the hall outside his office. A few weeks later I arranged for a moving company to transport my father's papers to Mississippi. The movers charged by weight. Their estimate of Dad's archive was eighteen hundred pounds. My inheritance.

Chapter Ten

AN INCREASING concern was my father's ashes. They still sat on the bookshelf where we'd put them after the memorial. The family hadn't settled on a plan, then we procrastinated as other priorities arose. One morning I awoke to thunder, followed by the pounding of rain against the windows. I was momentarily disoriented. I thought I was a kid and glanced about for my brother, undergoing a surge of anxiety that we were late for school. The remnants of a bad dream fled in fragmentary images, followed by the awareness of reality. I was in my childhood room, my father was dead, and I had a twelve-hour workday ahead of me.

The house was silent, my wife still asleep, my mother in the living room. I took coffee outside, where the shadows in the tree line glistened black. Every surface was a prism displaying the softened green of June. It was rainbow weather, but they were hard to spot among the hills. The air was a pane of lead—as my young son once said, not a sky in the cloud.

I finished my coffee and entered the house. Mom came into the kitchen, moving in a determined way, with an expression I recognized as secret satisfaction. I enjoyed seeing her this way. It was familiar, the way she'd always been: purposeful and private. The past few weeks had been hard, and she'd behaved with emotional distance, an armor to grief. She looked at me and spoke quietly. "I took care of your father's ashes."

Mom had decided the backyard was appropriate but worried the heavy ash might kill the grass. Equally bothersome was the prospect of wind blowing them onto the neighbor's land or into the gravel driveway, where she might inadvertently roll over them in the car. Mom had been waiting for a morning such as this. The chill air had been very still when she woke up. She could feel weather coming. Her plan was to scatter the remains just before the rain dampened the ashes and held them in place.

Earlier she'd sat on an outdoor swing beneath a canopy, drinking coffee and reading a magazine, alert to the barometric shifts in the atmosphere. At the first slight sprinkling of rain, she emptied the plastic box. It took longer than she'd expected, and the ashes didn't really scatter. Just as she finished, there was a bellow of thunder, and hard rain fell. She hurried back inside, her timing impeccable.

I nodded and refilled my coffee, wondering if the clap of thunder had been the same one that woke me. Was it coincidence or metaphysics? Or maybe all metaphysics is nothing but coincidence to which we assign meaning after the fact. It didn't matter. I asked her where the ashes were.

"Want to see?"

I nodded and followed her outside and across the narrow strip of land, scraped flat a hundred years before to form a yard I'd mowed as a child. Erosion had brought the steep slope six feet closer to the house. The hill itself was going over the hill. Mom led me to the edge of the yard. A few feet past the grass, she pointed to several clumps of ash, solidified by the rain into dark gray mounds.

"Well," I said, "it's not going to blow around the yard."

"No, it won't."

"How'd you pick this spot?"

"It's where your father always peed."

We stood there gazing at the rain-pocked hummocks of ash. I put my arm around my mother, unsure what to do or say. My siblings weren't coming back to the house. Nobody else would ever know where the ashes were. In time they'd make their way down the hill to the rain gully, merge with Triplett Creek, flow into the Licking River, drain to the Ohio River, join the Mississippi River, and progress south to the Gulf of Mexico and the Atlantic Ocean. It was a long trip. Part of him would make it.

Rain began falling again. Mom went back in the house. After a few minutes I did, too. Mom handed me a paper sack. Inside was the last of Dad's ashes, sealed in a rolled-up plastic sandwich bag. She made a joke that it resembled a nickel bag of pot, and I told her it had been a long time since she bought pot. She tipped her head and said, "I don't think I ever bought any. People just gave it to me. I thought it was so cool."

I looked at the bag in my palm. My father kept getting reduced, subdivided into packets. I was reminded of a battle scene in the movie *Monty Python and the Holy Grail*. King Arthur cuts off the arms and legs of the Black Knight, leaving him a limbless trunk, still trying to fight. Though I didn't want the leftover scraps of my father in a snack bag, I had to safeguard them. I was tired of it all—the house, the decisions, the porn, and now a nickel bag of ash. Standing in the kitchen and holding the remains of my father's remains, I had nowhere to take my irritation. My wife was exhausted, my mother slightly lost. At night they drank and tried to laugh.

The movers were coming at the end of the week, and we were behind on preparations. I set aside my feelings. It wasn't difficult. I hadn't cried, hadn't allowed myself to feel sorrow. There was simply too much to do. I went upstairs and tucked the Baggie in my suitcase. I still had boxes to fill, arrangements to make. We were low on packing tape. The gutters needed cleaning. I had to cancel the phone, talk to a lawyer, pay final bills. I could mourn later, be irritated later.

I'd spent the summer organizing everything into two groups: one for Mom's new place, a duplex in Oxford, Mississippi, and the rest bound for my house a few miles away in the country. Her load was furniture, clothes, and kitchen goods, while mine was Dad's desk, books, guns, and porn. I walked the rooms of my childhood home one last time, knowing I might never see them again. Empty, it was no longer Dad's house. I saw it as my parents had in 1964— the broad staircase, beautiful woodwork, and turn-of-the-century light fixtures. The living room seemed enormous without bulky furniture, centered around a fireplace with a mahogany mantel and carved posts. A good home for kids.

My father chopped firewood every day until age sixty, primarily using a long-handled double-bit ax. For tough hardwood, he resorted to a heavy maul. Dad stored the tools outside, exposed to weather, which rendered them worthless. I intended to keep his ax. The chipped blade was dull and rusted. I loved the hickory handle, split at least twice and crudely repaired with small nails, ragged duct tape, and wire as loose as bangles on a wrist. I knew my father had made these repairs, because my mother would have known to use screws for the wood. She'd have wrapped individual pieces of wire instead of one long piece destined to unravel quickly. The ax represented a part of my father separate from all other aspects—the outdoors. Splitting wood was the only activity I ever witnessed him doing outside, and, more important, the only task he'd ever let me help with.

My initial job was to gather pieces of bark to use as kindling. As I got older, I hauled armloads of firewood to the house. Next I graduated to placing a log upright on the chopping block, turning it in just the right way for Dad to see a knot. At age ten, I wielded a hatchet to trim small branches off the logs and split softwood for kindling.

Dad talked as he worked, calling each log a warrior, describing his combat. A heavy piece of oak with multiple hidden knots was a log that fought back. A stroke that split the log cleanly at a single blow was a beheading. Bark was blood. Chips were body parts. If he misaligned his aim and cut off a small strip of wood that flew across the yard, he said his opponent had thrown a dagger. This was partly for my entertainment, but it went deeper for Dad. As I watched him split log after log, sweat running down his face, vapor puffing from his mouth, I understood that he had entered an illusory realm in which he was determined to defeat an army of soldiers one by one. His competence increased as the foes became more real in his imagination. It was important that I remain silent, a squire to the knight. Afterward, Dad set the ax head on the ground and leaned on the handle, breathing hard from exertion. He stared at the plain of battle with an expression of triumph.

My car contained guns, bundles of cash I'd found hidden about the house, and boxes of vintage pornography. If I got pulled over and searched, I'd probably go to jail. If I had a wreck, money and porn would litter the interstate, mixed with my funeral suit, my grandfather's rifle, a shotgun, three hundred rounds of ammunition, the remnants of my father's ashes, and whatever was left of me.

The last items to pack were Dad's ax, the old maul, and a broad-sword that wouldn't fit in a box. Without plan or forethought, I carried them to the edge of the hill. Mom had cast the ashes in three distinct areas, now little more than gray streaks in the ground. A few tiny piles of sediment lay beneath blown leaves. I pushed the sword blade through the ash into the soft earth and pounded the hilt with the maul. I did the same with the ax. I placed the heavy maul on a pile of brush. I'd acted on impulse and now spoke without filter. "I know you were curious about the afterlife. Just in case there is one, I figure you're here and know what I'm doing. The sword is for Andy. The ax is for John Cleve. The maul is for Turk Winter. I figure you'd appreciate this. Okay, Dad. See you."

A flash of silver metal glittered on the ground. I picked it up and wiped it on my pants to clean the dirt. It was a stainless-steel disc used by the crematorium to identify the corpse and later placed with the ashes. Number 179. An odd number. Square-free. A safe prime.

Dad.

Chapter Eleven

MOM IS circumspect about details of her early years in Haldeman, stressing only that she was never unhappy: "That was where I was and I accepted it." I can't imagine it was easy—she'd grown up in a city of more than fifty thousand people, in a tightly knit community of working-class Irish, with many relatives. In Haldeman she lived on a dirt road in the woods with four young children and no friends or family nearby. Dad was gone every day and many nights, working as a salesman.

To a large extent, my mother was on her own in a foreign environment. I was Mom's sole source of aid, her little helper. She depended on me, and soon my siblings did, as well. Mom was the shepherd and I was the loyal guard dog, protecting my ragtag flock of three. Mom often said she liked it best when I got sick instead of my siblings because I didn't need her ministrations, preferring to go off alone like a dog and lick my wounds.

Naturally we all wanted my mother's attention, but they received it more directly than I did. On me she bestowed a special appreciation for daily assistance and making her laugh. It was less a mother/son relationship and more like that of a senior and junior partner in a shared enterprise. There was a bliss to our closeness as we worked together to get through the day. Mom and I lived in fear of Dad, but each of us knew he loved us best. He remained in love with her throughout his life. I was his favorite child, the golden boy of the family. In his eyes, I was always firstborn son, prince to the king, a successor.

I spent very little private time with my father, which made those experiences intensely meaningful. When I was thirteen, he took me on a long drive in his car. He was extremely quiet, which was unusual. A few times he began speaking, then faltered and trailed away in a mumble. After an hour or so we returned home and he gave me a pamphlet on frog reproduction. In retrospect I understand that he had tasked himself with explaining the birds and bees to his son but was unable to follow through.

In 1971 he took me to the movie *Billy Jack*. He'd seen it the week before and believed its message of a lone man fighting social injustice would convey a valuable lesson. I was thrilled that he wanted to spend time with me. What I most recall is my father's pre-movie commentary on behavior in a theater, which began with the choice of viewing position. Never sit down front, where you'd have to strain your neck looking up. Don't sit in the back, because that was where people talked. The middle was no good, because most viewers sat there and you'd be hemmed in. The best seat was three quarters toward the rear, near the aisle, behind and to the side of a couple. No one would sit beside them and block your view. I listened attentively, and we entered the theater. We were the only people there.

He whispered his instructions after we sat. Never buy popcorn, which was overpriced and stale. If you bought candy in a bag, it was best to open it in a swift rip, because the long, slow sound of tearing paper was distracting. Boxes of candy presented another problem, particularly jawbreakers. You had to open the box in a way that allowed it to be reclosed. If the structure of the box prevented that, it was crucial to hold the box upright to avoid spilling the candy. The issue was not waste but disturbance. The sound of jawbreakers rolling down the sloped theater floor was deeply offensive to Dad.

The movie impressed me with its use of the word "fuck" and a blurred image of a female breast. The character Billy Jack used martial arts to fight for the rights of hippies and Native Americans. After the movie we went to the restroom and stood at the urinal. Dad told me that I was an alpha male. I nodded. He asked if I knew what that meant and I shook my head. He explained that an alpha male was more or less the boss dog of any outfit. It meant that beautiful women liked to talk to you, and men naturally looked to you for orders. He said that beta males were plumbers, doctors, mechanics, and engineers. Below them were delta males, which included everyone else.

He explained the three types of alpha—I was an alpha three and Billy Jack was an alpha two. Dad waited long enough for me to understand that I was supposed to ask who was an alpha one, which I did.

"Me," he said, and zipped his pants.

I went to the sink, but he told me I didn't need to wash up.

"Alphas don't piss on their hands."

Years later Dad fondly recalled *Billy Jack* as the last movie we saw together. I didn't have the heart to tell him it was the only one.

Chapter Twelve

LIKE MOST young couples, my parents responded to situations as well as they could with limited information, conforming to convention and social expectation. They were good Catholics, both virgins when they married at age twenty-three.

Mom was a McCabe and a McCarney, from Lexington's tough Irish-Catholic community. Her grandfather, a career bartender, was known for having shot and killed a drunken customer. Other family members were bookies and gamblers. Her uncle embalmed the great racehorse Man o' War. Her great-uncle studied for the priesthood, and her aunt became a nun. In high school, Mom began caring for her ill mother, a responsibility that steadily increased for four years. As eldest daughter, she took over the household—preparing meals for her sister and father—and began working at a bank.

At age twenty-two, she met Dad at a Catholic Youth Organization dance. On their subsequent first date Dad wore a suit and took her to the nicest restaurant in town. She was flattered by his attention—he was handsome, funny, and very smart. He behaved like a gentleman, which meant "not trying any funny business." They were the same age, born a few months apart. At seventeen, Mom had lost her mother. Dad's father had died the same year. They'd endured loss and economic deprivation, but they also shared a strong hope for the future, motivated by the prosperity and enthusiasm of the 1950s. Ten months after meeting, they were married and remained deeply in love the rest of their lives. I never heard them argue or even disagree.

Dad sold products for Procter & Gamble, supplying to small country stores, then coming home and writing late into the night. My mother read Dr. Spock and cooked from cans. In the evenings they drank martinis. Energetic and ambitious, my father moved into the insurance business and was offered a promotion selling policies to college students in the eastern hills. Not yet thirty, he related well to undergraduates. With three kids and a pregnant wife, he could bring his own circumstances to bear in a sales pitch: *If something happened to me, what would my wife do? Who would feed my kids? You should ask yourself the same questions.*

In 1963, weary from driving a hundred miles a day, Dad moved the family to a small rental house in the conservative town of Morehead. My parents strove for upward mobility in a place that offered little in the way of a toehold. They socialized with college professors and doctors. Mom was intimidated by their levels of education but learned to hide it behind an increasingly polished patina of appropriate conversation. Dad was contemptuous of medical personnel, whom he referred to as "body plumbers." He believed himself far more intelligent than the professors and considered a Ph.D. nothing more than a union card to teach.

A year later Dad learned about a home for sale ten miles away, located on a ridge in the former mining community of

Haldeman, population two hundred. The deceased town founder, L. P. Haldeman, had built a pair of fine homes and used the smaller house to entertain while living in the big one. His primary residence was for sale. It was a large house, solidly built fifty years before. The asking price was low due to a significant drawback. Situated at the bottom of the hill directly below the house was a factory that manufactured charcoal. The kilns produced a toxic smoke.

Dad drove the family out of town, following a creek fed by rain gullies clawed into the hillside. Gleaming railroad tracks ran on a raised bed of fist-sized gravel. There were no road signs. We crossed railroad tracks and immediately smelled smoke. In the sole wide spot available, lodged tight to the base of the main hill, was the enormous charcoal factory, pumping black smoke into the sky. Dad left the blacktop for a steep dirt road that ascended a hill beneath a canopy of trees. Rocks bounced against the car. At the top of the hill, Dad stopped in a flat spot where six ridges merged like spokes to a wagon wheel. Surrounding the crossroads were more trees, their bottom leaves coated with charcoal dust. My parents consulted directions and followed a dirt road that faded to a set of ruts with grass growing in the center. At the end of the road stood the house, surrounded by the Daniel Boone National Forest.

The windows lacked curtains and the interior was dim. Without furnishings, the house reverberated from our footsteps and echoing voices. There were three rooms downstairs and three bedrooms upstairs. It had been built with indoor plumbing, rare for the early 1900s in the hills, and had a bathroom on each floor.

Mom wandered as if in a trance, her belly swollen with child, exclaiming again and again how much space there was in the house. Dad strode with purpose. The house was just what a young man needed for a growing family. He was not concerned that his wife had lived all her life in Lexington and had no idea how to raise children in a rural setting. He didn't mind not knowing anyone in the community. He ignored the empty mines, old train tracks, trash-filled creeks, and charcoal smoke. He didn't know Haldeman had the highest rate of unemployment and illiteracy in the county, among the highest in the state. Less than a mile away was a bootlegger, which spawned gunplay, arson, and drag races that often ended in spectacular wrecks. None of it mattered to Dad. The large house was a long way from the log cabin of his youth. He bought Mr. Haldeman's home and lived there for fifty years.

Late at night after everyone else went to bed, my father listened for evidence of Mr. Haldeman's ghost. At the slightest creak, Dad spoke aloud: *Hello, is that you?* He believed that directly addressing a spirit would provoke a response. Even as a child, I found it odd that he put forth such effort to communicate with the ethereal world but not his kids. He was always disappointed that the house remained silent, that the ghost ignored him.

During the 1960s, Appalachia experienced the biggest outmigration in its history due to economics. Hundreds of families moved to Michigan and Ohio for work. This diaspora made room for people such as my father, who needed a great deal of psychic space. We were the first new family to arrive in Haldeman in more than thirty years. Many of our neighbors lacked conventional plumbing. They grew subsistence gardens, raised hogs and chickens, and hunted for food. Some families grew a small tobacco crop for cash and gathered ginseng from the woods to sell. Many received welfare assistance. No one went to college, and very few finished high school. It was not uncommon for men to go about armed. The sound of gunfire became as normal to my ears as that of barking dogs. I learned to discern the differences in pitch among shotgun, pistol, and rifle.

My parents enjoyed their lack of local history and began severing relations with their own families. I grew up without direct benefit of cousins, uncles, aunts, or grandparents. Relatives were what other people had, not us. Mom and Dad scorned our neighbors as ignorant and unsophisticated. They taught my siblings and me to consider ourselves better than the families who surrounded us, the children with whom we played, and the culture we came to identify as our own. My experience was similar to that of children of career diplomats from the colonial era—we lived in the big house, we had extra money, we mingled with the locals but never fit in. We even spoke a different language, what my father called "the Queen's English," instead of the grammatically incorrect dialect of the hills. Other kids learned to hunt and fish; I learned to speak properly.

The surrounding hills held rich veins of dense, flinty clay, ideal for manufacturing sturdy firebrick to line blast furnaces for steel mills. In 1903 Lunsford Pitt Haldeman founded the Kentucky Fire Brick Company and hired men to lay narrow-gauge rail for mules to haul hand-dug clay to the brick plant. Business flourished through the 1920s, with the brickyard being the largest employer in the region, producing sixty thousand bricks per day, each stamped "Haldeman Ky." The company town had brick roads, a public garden, a barbershop, a baseball diamond, and a train depot. There was a tennis court, several horseshoe pits, and a neatly cropped field for playing croquet. Workers were paid in a combination of cash and scrip, a form of credit against wages that could be exchanged only at the high-priced Company Store.

In the 1950s, General Refractories purchased the old brick factory and converted its kilns to manufacture charcoal. This was accomplished by burning railroad ties that were heavily soaked in creosote, an oily liquid obtained from coal tar and used as a wood preservative. The resultant char was sent north, chipped into briquettes, bagged, and sold for summer barbecues across the nation. The constant heavy smoke increased Haldeman fatalities among the elderly and infants. Everyone coughed. At night the humidity produced fog that blended with the smoke to create an opaque smog that car headlights couldn't penetrate. Dad walked ahead of the car with a flashlight to illuminate the way for Mom to drive. Storekeepers in Morehead could identify us by the acrid smell of smoke on our clothing, and they used it as a means to discriminate against us. Haldeman people were at the bottom of a pecking order that didn't start very high. Plus, we literally stank.

The factory stood two hundred yards from the grade school. Smoke drifted through the air as I walked to school, obscuring the woods like a lethal morning mist that never lifted. In 1968 my parents organized a small group called Struggle Opposing Smog, or SOS. To get attention, they withheld their children from the first week of school, drawing national media coverage for the unique boycott. Special devices were fastened to the smokestacks to measure the amount of particulates spewing forth. After two days every gauge broke, with their final readings listing higher pollution rates than those in Detroit. The charcoal factory shut down. Some people admired my parents for their effort, while others resented the loss of employment. None could deny that the quality of air had improved.

Most rural childhoods are very isolated, but due to Haldeman's past as a company town, people lived in clusters along creeks and ridges. The culture of the hills had long maintained the vestiges of the eighteenth-century pioneer mentality: self-sufficiency, hunting game for food, and a disregard for conventional law. Ten boys near my age lived within walking distance through the woods. We roamed the hills on foot and later on bicycles, careening our battered bikes along game trails and footpaths, plunging down steep hills. We were reckless and ragtag, fearless and rough, perpetually cut and bruised. Cheap army-surplus shirts from the Vietnam War were ideal for the woods. The tightly woven fabric repelled water and thorns. A couple of us were always limping, our unprotected faces bruised and cut. Occasionally I had two black eyes, a source of pride, since anyone could have merely one.

We found junked cars from the thirties with trees growing through the windows, foundations of houses filled with garbage, and dozens of empty holes in the ground. The woods were full of bricks, all stamped with the name of our community. We ate in one another's homes, helped with chores, and shared gloves in winter. Our lives knew no boundaries save the distance we could travel on foot and still be home by dark. We loved one another in a pure way that none of us was loved at home.

I grew up in the shadow of a complex history mythologized by the faded glory days of a lost town. The popular story is that L. P. Haldeman did everything in his power to take care of his workers. He made sure that even the most poverty-stricken children living in dilapidated company shacks received a Christmas gift of fruit. One story that demonstrated his compassion was about a man who died on the job, leaving a family with no means of support. The oldest boy was thirteen. Mr. Haldeman directed that a special stool be constructed for the boy to stand on so he could work in his father's place all day.

Employees received approximately ten dollars a week for working seventy hours. In 1934 they organized Local Union No. 510 and went on strike. The men wanted more money for shorter hours. Mr. Haldeman refused to meet with union representatives. Court documents quoted him as saying: "I will shut the damn thing down, and let it sit there, and possibly the rust will eat it up."

The Rowan County judge sent a detachment of the National Guard to the brickyard, along with seventy-five local "deputies." Plant operations resumed. Thirty-six men were denied a return to work. All of their names had appeared on a secret list obtained by a private investigator working for the company. In 1938 Kentucky Fire Brick lost a lawsuit filed on behalf of those men. Incensed at being legally forced to reinstate his workers, Mr. Haldeman sold the company to U.S. Steel. Included in the sale were the elementary school, parts of the railroad, a blacktopped portion of the old Main Road, several houses, vast acres of mined-out land, and in a very real sense, the people who lived there. Able-bodied men with families moved elsewhere for jobs. Most of the people who stayed had a disability, owned their own land outright, or received a military pension.

The surnames of the men named in the 1938 lawsuit were as follows: Adkins, Bailey, Christian, Davis, Eldridge, Evans, Glover, Hall, Hogge, Lewis, Messer, Oney, Parker, Pettit, Rakes, Sparks, Sturgell, Stinson, Sparkman, Stamper, Sammon, Stewart, Thomas, White, and Wilson. I recognize every name, having grown up with their descendants.

My understanding of the town's decline was simple—ungrateful workers were to blame. I didn't realize until much later that all the profits from Kentucky Fire Brick went out of state and that families didn't own the mineral rights to their property. Lunsford Pitt Haldeman was the scion of a wealthy Ohio family who inherited Kentucky land. Under pressure to become an entrepreneur, he hired a childhood friend to run the company while he stayed in Ohio.

My hometown was nothing more than a business enterprise.

When its profitability began to wane, L. P. Haldeman quickly rid himself of the responsibility. He never actually lived in the town that bore his name, and certainly not in our house. He left no spirit for my father to talk with. But like a ghost, his unseen presence was strongly felt. The remaining evidence of the despotic town founder is his last name on thousands of bricks, each one as chipped and battered as the people he abandoned.

Chapter Thirteen

THE KITCHEN had an electric stove with an array of buttons for controlling heat—extra-low, low, medium, medium-high, high, extra-high. Pressing one button automatically popped free the others. The newfangled space-age system fascinated me, and I discerned a relationship between the letters on the buttons and the intensity of heat. My mother explained the alphabet. At age five I taught myself to read other kitchen items: sugar, flour, salt, Jif, Kraft, Velveeta, Frigidaire, and Osterizer.

During the 1930s, the Works Progress Administration built my elementary school from huge blocks of sandstone transported by rail from nearby Bluestone Quarry. As with all structures in Appalachia, geography dictated location. The school sat in a wide holler flanked by steep hills. Our playground was half an acre of rock and dirt with no basketball hoop, monkey bars, or swing set. Our only rules were to stay out of the creek and the road.

We began each day by pledging allegiance to the flag, then reciting the Lord's Prayer. For the next ten minutes we stood by our desks and sang patriotic songs and hymns. I took everything literally and was a serious though naive thinker. We often sang the spiritual "He's Got the Whole World in His Hands." I believed this was actual truth, that God was a giant, big enough to hold the Earth in his palm. The darkness of night was a result of God putting the world in his pants pocket. Stars perplexed me. They appeared to be holes in the fabric of God's pants, allowing the entrance of light. I believed God's clothing would be better than mine. My mother washed our family's clothes once a week, and it made sense that God's mom did, too. Therefore, I concluded, stars were evidence of a tissue in God's pocket that went through the wash. He was all-powerful and all-knowing, but his mother wasn't. It was she who forgot to remove the tissue from God's pants.

I applied a similar logic to the existence of a water fountain in school. At age six, I'd never seen one before. A classmate explained that the schoolhouse had a big well under it to supply the water. His thick accent stretched the word "well" to sound like "whale." My understanding was that living in the earth beneath the school was a whale the size of the one that swallowed Jonah. When its blowhole spewed, pipes captured the water and ran it to the drinking fountain. One day during lunch break, I tried to crawl under the school and look for the whale. The principal caught me and I dutifully explained my mission. He was amused, telling me I had a big imagination for such a little fellow. A few years later I understood why my classmate had been so excited by plumbing. His family had no water at their house. One of his chores was to draw water from a well and haul it home.

After school I walked a creek, then climbed the dirt road to a shortcut path through the heavy woods. For the first few years I rushed home. Mom met me at the back door with a hug and a snack. My brother and sisters were overjoyed by my return, as if they'd feared I was gone for good.

My memory of fourth grade is very strong, perhaps because I began writing and drawing in earnest then. From that year I have four short stories and two essays. It was also the first year I began keeping a daily journal, small, with a psychedelic design on the cover appropriate to the year 1968. Possibly the act of documenting my perceptions enabled my memory to retain greater clarity. Maybe my interest in the world increased, or my senses reached a new plateau, or the compulsion to observe was born. In any case, it was the earliest period from which I can remember long sections of my life, as if the act of recollection itself had become a narrative.

On the first day of fourth grade, the teacher distributed textbooks to use throughout the year. I read them all in a week and spent the next nine months reading books, drawing pictures, and writing stories. Teachers often reprimanded me for "disturbing my neighbors," which seemed an odd term, something people on the hill did with rifles and dogs.

The school lacked specialized instruction for children with developmental disabilities. The principal put them in the classroom that was appropriate to their level. The term used for them was "retarded" and included autism, Downs syndrome, products of incest and poor prenatal diet. In fourth grade we had such a boy named Carson, who had been held back so often he was gripped by advanced puberty. Bigger and stronger than the rest of us, he spoke in a series of unintelligible lisping grunts. He couldn't read or write. Due to his impulsive behavior, Carson's desk sat in a corner at the front of the classroom. No one dared touch it. A favorite prank was to trip someone, forcing the victim to grab Carson's desk for support, thereby receiving a quick transmission of cooties. Carson seldom attended school.

When frustrated, angry, or merely irritated, teachers beat students with wooden paddles. Strangely, our fourth-grade teacher didn't believe in hitting children. Her punishments included staying in the classroom during lunch recess or sitting in Carson's seat for half an hour. One day I made three paper airplanes, each smaller than the other, and lodged them within the crease that formed the fuselage of the largest craft. My idea was to send them aloft together and re-create the three stages of a rocket launch. Instead, I was caught by the teacher at the very moment of throwing the planes. She banished me to Carson's desk for the rest of the year.

I placed a textbook on the seat as a sanitizing device, fearful that some aspect of Carson would be contagious. I sat with rigid posture. The desktop held a patina of hieroglyphs representing years of student boredom—names and initials gouged into the wood, blackened by grime and pencil, shellacked over, then cobwebbed again with another generation's imprint. By the end of the following day, I appreciated the benefits of my new situation. The desk sat beside the door, allowing me to be last in the room and first out. I faced the blackboard with my back to the class, providing a personal space and privacy that was absent at home. For the first time I came to love school.

During winter, icicles glittered on the cliffs. Low branches dumped snow on me as I walked to school. Warm weather finally arrived. Pink and white dogwoods dotted the hills. Forsythia bushes bloomed bright yellow. Carson came to school. The teacher ordered me back to my original spot. I locked my ankles around the wooden legs of Carson's desk, gripped the seat, and reminded her that she'd ordered me to sit there until the end of the year. Exasperated by my defiance, she sent Carson to my seat. Within half an hour someone provoked him into an unruly act. The teacher made him stand. She pushed my former desk to the other corner in the front of the room and told Carson to sit there. Our class finished the spring semester with the smartest kid and the dumbest kid sitting in opposite corners, yin and yang, each of us in the other's seats. Combined, we made a single average student.

It would be easy to criticize the teacher's method of discipline, but she was gentle with Carson, possibly the first person who was. Intimidated by his size, teachers often sent him to the principal's office for a paddling. He calmly lay prone on the floor, frustrating the principal, who believed it was a trick to avoid punishment.

Many years later, Carson's cousin told me that he lived with his grandmother, who suffered from an unrepaired cleft palate, which rendered her articulations impossible to understand. Carson had copied her speech since birth. Before beating him, she made him lie on the floor because it was easier for her to hit him from a chair. After school Carson chopped wood and hauled water instead of doing homework. He was shy and illiterate, and never learned to talk plainly, but there was nothing at all wrong with his mind.

By age ten I read a book a day, two if it rained. In summer I waited for the bookmobile to trundle up the dirt road in first gear, driven by a young female volunteer. She wore a headband and patched bell-bottom trousers, her neck draped with beads. My intense feelings for her were unnameable: I couldn't look at her, could barely talk. I had a persistent fantasy of driving around the country with her, living in the bookmobile, and reading forever. One day the truck didn't arrive and I never saw her again.

I'd already read my father's holdings of pre–World War II fare from his own childhood: *The Bobbsey Twins, Billy Whiskers, The Hardy Boys, Nancy Drew,* and *Tom Swift.* I then began his collection of adventure novels by Edgar Rice Burroughs, Robert E. Howard, Alexandre Dumas, Robert Louis Stevenson, and Daniel Defoe. I spent an entire Saturday utilizing a short ladder and a long rope to climb a crabapple tree and nail a board to a fork of limbs. There I could sit and read, ensconced away from my siblings. Bees circled my head, but I understood that if I didn't fear them, they left me alone.

Reading wasn't an attempt to educate myself. It was my chief escape from a world that, although gorgeous in landscape and rich with mountain culture, didn't provide what I needed—the promise of adventure, a life beyond the perimeter of hills. I often fantasized that I'd been adopted and had mysterious powers such as flying or teleportation. Books offered the promise of a world in which misfits like me could flourish. Within the pages of a novel, I was unafraid: of my father, of dogs, snakes, and the bully across the creek; of older boys who drove hot rods close enough to make me jump in the ditch; of armed men parked near the bootlegger. If there had been a movie theater or an art gallery, I'd have found solace there. In Appalachia, oddly enough, I had literature.

A new library opened in Morehead. Every Saturday my mother drove to town for groceries, dropped me at the library, and picked me up later. The library had a four-book limit for each person. My solution was to acquire cards in the names of my siblings and the family dog, which allowed me twenty books per week. My first favorite novel was *Harriet the Spy* by Louise Fitzhugh. The primary circumstances of Harriet's life could not be further removed from mine—she lived in New York City with a nanny and a cook. I'd always identified with protagonists whose adventures stemmed from external circumstances, fantasizing about being Tom Sawyer, Sherlock Holmes, or John Carter. With Harriet M. Welsch, I found someone who created her own internal drama through the recording of her observations. She was more real to me than Tarzan, her life grounded in ways similar to mine. Largely ignored by her parents, she was a loner who wore jeans and sneakers and carried a pocketknife—the same as me. She wandered her neighborhood, interacting with people at a slight remove—exactly as I did. She kept a notebook and spare pens with her at all times.

After finishing the book, I used my allowance to buy a notebook and pens, my first purchase of anything other than comic books and model cars. I resolved to carry pen and paper for the rest of my life and write down my observations, a habit I've maintained for nearly fifty years.

To prepare for high school, we began changing classes in the fifth grade. The math and spelling teacher had a homemade paddle, long and skinny, with a carved handle. She employed it more than anyone, always on boys. An odd tradition emerged of signing your name on the paddle after she beat you. I never understood this and refused to sign it, although she hit me often. She administered punishment in the hall, where the errant student leaned forward and placed his hands against the wall. She stood behind him and swung her paddle as if it were a baseball bat.

In spelling class, our weekly assignment was to define twenty spelling words. I jotted down the answers rapidly and turned them in. The teacher discounted them, saying that I was supposed to copy definitions from the dictionary. I told her that was boring, since I already knew the words. She scoffed at that, telling me to prove it by writing a story in which I used all the words correctly. If I made a mistake, I'd get a paddling.

The next week's spelling list included "minute," which I dutifully included in a story about medieval jousting. The two knights were Sir Christophoro and Sir Robbiano, sworn enemies seeking to please the king. A boy named Robbie lived near me, on the same ridge but across a narrow holler. His father bullied him and Robbie bullied me. He once held the low branch of a tree in such a fashion that when he released it, the branch sprang through the air and hit me in the face. It hurt badly and left a mark for days. Robbie defeated me in real life, but in my story, Sir Christophoro slaughtered Sir Robbiano without mercy.

My first story for spelling class included this line: "Sir Christophoro's wound was minute." The teacher was delighted by my apparent misuse of the word, suggesting to the class that I was trying to get attention. I protested, claiming that "minute" was correct. In an attempt to shame me before the class, she told me to fetch the Wordbook and look up "minute." I read aloud the second definition, in which "minute" meant trivial or insignificant. She accused me of lying. When I showed her the dictionary, her expression revealed to me the enormous power of language. The short stories I subsequently wrote in spelling class forged a link between the act of writing and rebellion. Narrative was a weapon against the world, more effective than Sir Christophoro's sword.

By sixth grade, I'd depleted the school library, an area of the lunchroom cordoned off by a flimsy row of fabric-covered partitions, and turned to my father's personal library. He owned the fifty-four-volume hardbound set of Great Books of the Western World, two sets of encyclopedias, and a collection of scholarly works on religion, psychology, ancient history, military campaigns, and sexuality. The shelves also held popular literature and science fiction. I read constantly with no oversight or guidance and a disregard for content. They were just books: Mark Twain, Sigmund Freud, Homer, George Bernard Shaw, Booth Tarkington, Euripides, Thorne Smith, Leo Tolstoy, Carl Jung, Charles Darwin, Damon Runyon, Aristotle, Thomas Aquinas, and so forth.

I was reading over my head but didn't know it because no one told me so. I didn't discriminate or evaluate. Each book carried the same weight, equal in its value. The more I read, the more I wanted to learn. As I gained information about the world, I realized I'd never be able to read everything and would eventually be compelled to pick and choose. Until then, I merely absorbed narrative and idea, finishing Shakespeare and picking up Heinlein, dipping into Machiavelli and then Tolkein. I was like a blind man trying to stay warm in winter, grabbing the nearest piece of wood, unable to discern hardwood or soft, concerned only with maintaining the hot steady fire that consumed everything in reach.

Reading and writing helped me defeat the tedium of school, but I continued to be a discipline problem. I can't recall what led to my final paddling in eighth grade. Escorted by my teacher into the hall, I expected the usual punishment of three licks. She placed me against the wall and hit me six times very hard and very fast. The first three I was able to withstand, but after six, I knew I was going to cry. The prospect of public mortification when I returned to the classroom was overwhelming. Instead of crying, I began to laugh, which served as a release much the same as tears. The teacher interpreted my mirth as being directed at her. She hit me six more times. I began moving away prior to her last two strikes, and she got them in quicker, the last one hitting my upper thigh. I spun to her, pain fueling my anger. Her face was red, and tears streamed from her eyes. Utterly discombobulated, I left school. I stayed in the woods until everyone had gone home, then went back for my homework and lunch sack. The next day I learned that I'd set a school record with twelve licks, the most for a single paddling. The teacher never looked me in the eye again.

A month later I graduated from Haldeman Grade School as the 1972 valedictorian, the apex of my academic career. The lesson I'd learned best was the value of concealing my intelligence.

Chapter Fourteen

MY PARENTS were rock-solid members of the so-called Silent Generation, born into the Great Depression and coming of age during World War II. They married in 1957, determined to maintain a facade of proper behavior, grooming, and appearance. Mom had learned to touch-type with the goal of being a secretary but really wanted to be a mother and a homemaker. My father had taken the appropriate steps of a proper citizen—active in church, president of his college fraternity and the Newman Club, an officer in Big Brothers of America. He joined the Toastmasters Club to improve his public speaking and became a member of the Kiwanis Club for business connections.

Throughout the 1960s, Dad wrote at night and on weekends, producing eighteen short stories and nine novels. He worked in the unfinished basement, facing a tiny black-and-white television set that received one channel. The walls leaked with every rain. Tangled tree roots caused the septic tank to periodically reverse its flow into the basement. On Saturday and Sunday he sat at the dining room table with an old manual typewriter. He worked with astonishing speed, slamming the carriage return several times per minute. The machine vibrated the table, which made his ashtray and water glass travel randomly about the surface. At least once a day, he knocked the carriage into his glass and sent water flying across fresh manuscript pages. Dad would curse mightily, aiming his rage at anyone nearby. By age eight, I began devoting my weekends to the outdoors. I needed solitude as much as my father did.

Dad began using lowercase letters for his formal name in every instance. His books were by "andrew j. offutt," and his letters were signed "andy." The insurance company he formed was "andrew j. offutt associates." He told me the reason—he wanted to stand out from the crowd. "They'll remember me that way," he said. And he was right. By 1968 Dad operated insurance agencies in three towns, winning awards for his salesmanship and supervisory ability. He later told me that the movers and shakers in Kentucky politics, *the big boys in Frankfort,* were looking him over. He drove a four-door Mercedes-Benz, the only one in the county, and assembled an impeccable wardrobe of tailored suits and conservative ties. As he put it: "When you leave a place, you want people to remember that you were very well dressed, but not what you were wearing."

At age thirty-five he'd achieved his goals—social status, big house, nice car, his own business. He also felt snared by his values. He didn't like children. He made it clear to the family that he'd fathered kids due to Catholicism and resented the Church for the burden. The only planned birth was my brother. He wished he'd stopped at two. I spoke to my younger sisters privately, reassuring them that Dad loved them, he just didn't like religion.

Though highly successful as a businessman, Dad was frustrated and miserable. He slept poorly and never enough. He skipped breakfast and drank a viscous liquid called Metrecal for lunch. As soon as he came home, he dropped two tablets of Alka-Seltzer in a glass of water, then switched to beer. Since childhood, all he'd ever wanted to do was write. Now he had more ideas and less time, and he hated the life he'd dutifully built. He wanted a way out but wouldn't leave my mother. Instead, he spread his misery to the family. Because my father's abuse was verbal, I developed a kind of emotional telepathy. My role was to deflect and defuse with quick-witted comments that would lighten the prevailing mood. No one strained against Dad more than I did, but no one could make him laugh as readily. He needed me in that capacity. I learned to be funny.

In the mid-sixties two significant events influenced the future of our family. My mother recalls Dad sitting in the living room reading a pornographic novel he'd bought through the mail. Dad hurled it across the room and said, "I can write better than this!" She suggested he do so. By 1969 he'd published five and had contracts for two more.

By then the full emergence of my permanent teeth had made a mess of my mouth, forming three rows of front teeth. The canines occupied first position. My incisors were directly behind them, followed by the lateral incisors. My smile led with fangs, then two rows of bigger teeth, producing the appearance of a miniature shark.

According to my mother, the condition of my mouth didn't matter to Dad, because his family were country people who let their teeth go. Since his early twenties, he'd worn a full set of dentures, upper and lower. For the first time in twelve years of marriage, Mom took a stand, insisting that she go to work and finance my orthodontic needs. With all the kids in school, she had the bulk of her days free. Dad spent most of his time unhappily driving between multiple offices for his insurance agency. He believed he could double his writing output with a full-time typist. If he quit his job to write, and Mom typed his manuscripts for submission, they'd make enough money to fix my teeth.

My parents were not brave people. Nor were they particularly bold in any way. Economic deprivation in childhood had taught them thrift and caution. They worked hard and played it safe. After a great deal of planning, my father made the most courageous decision of his life, the only risk he ever took—but it was enormous. At age thirty-six, with four kids, an uneducated wife, and a big mortgage, he decided to pursue his lifelong dream of being a professional writer.

My father's sudden presence in the house jarred the family in many ways. He went from being gone fifty hours a week to being in the house all the time. Home was now a place of business. He was *working,* which meant the house had to be quiet—no loud talking, laughing, or walking. We learned to move silently up and down the steps. Doors had to be eased shut or left open. The slightest sound startled Dad, who would yell. The steady clatter of his typewriter filled the house.

My mother changed her schedule, as well. She and Dad stayed in their closed bedroom until we left for school. Prior to this we'd had her to ourselves: Mom bathed us, fed us, kissed our scrapes, and soothed our feelings. Now she devoted herself to the needs of our father. She no longer met us after school with snacks and a hug. We didn't gain a father, we lost our mother.

Beginning at age twelve, my job was to get my siblings up and dressed, prepare their breakfast, then herd them to school along a path through the woods. This way, our parents could sleep undisturbed. Often my sister's asthma was very severe and I had to make a decision whether she'd attend school or not. Waking my parents was against the rules. My sister had a specific posture for breathing, a kind of leaning-forward crouch in bed, her head turned slightly to one side. I'd ask my sister to sit up and take a deep breath. If it seemed like too much of a struggle, I told her to stay home. I went to school and she lay in bed, striving to breathe, scared of Dad's reaction when he awoke. With each painful inhalation, she hoped the asthma attack would last long enough for him to wake up and understand it was serious.

My father's new home office, formerly my sisters' bedroom, had two windows and a closet. Bookshelves covered three walls from floor to ceiling. A massive walnut desk stood in the middle of the room. Manufactured in 1960, it was executive furniture intended to impress clients, a gift from Dad's boss during his insurance career. It served as an island, four feet wide and seven feet long, with narrow passageways on three sides. Beyond it, farthest from the door, ran a tight alley with a ladder-backed chair facing a tiny alcove that held a typewriter. No one was welcome.

My mother stood outside the door and waited for permission to enter, even after he had shouted a demand for coffee. I avoided communicating with Dad in his office. It was a multi-step process that began with tiptoeing to the door so as not to startle him. I tapped softly and waited for his acknowledgment, an interval that could run a few minutes. I wondered if he heard me, but I knew better than to knock again and risk arousing his ire. Dad regarded any intrusion as not merely a distraction but a form of disrespect and attack.

His response was always the same, a command: "Come." After being granted admittance, I eased the door open and approached the gigantic desk covered with books and papers. A rifle leaned in a corner. The smell of menthol cigarettes layered the room. Beyond the desk, filling the small space, was my glaring father. I anxiously stated my business. He responded curtly, then dismissed me by beginning to type. I was glad to be away, but sad that he didn't want me there.

On one occasion Dad summoned me to his fortlike office and motioned me to sit in a chair tucked into a corner and stacked with books. I hesitated until he told me to put the books on his desk.

This felt like a high honor—allowed to touch his goods and sit in a chair. I basked in the temporary attention of my father within the confines of his office. It's beyond my memory what was so important that he treated me this way, but I recall hoping that it signaled a shift in the nature of our relationship. As time passed, I understood that the incident had been an anomaly, that it meant the world to me but nothing to him.

Dad often joked that he was mentally ill, dismissing it as symptomatic of being a writer, the same as drinking. At the supper table, he'd loosen his upper and lower dentures with his tongue, shake his head back and forth to make the plastic scrape together, and tell the family that the sound was his brains rattling. In my late thirties, I understood that something was wrong with him, that he did suffer a genuine psychological malady. I didn't know what it was, but my response was to stop going home. I couldn't fix him.

The only correct perception of any situation was his. Disagreement sparked emotional combat and verbal abuse. It was incumbent upon his family to listen to him, agree with him, admire him, and give him attention bordering on awe. If Dad was enthralled by something—a movie, reincarnation, a book on UFOs, ancient Rome—we needed to be, too. Any disagreement was perceived as a terrible threat, and his response was swift and powerful: massive retaliation of a verbal nature. He never struck us or our mother, but we feared his anger, his belittling comments and inflictions of guilt.

My brother-in-law once remarked that it was amazing Dad lived as long as he did without getting punched out. I hadn't considered it before, but he was right. The reason was Dad's careful structuring of his life—he resisted entering any situation that he couldn't control. No one ever hit him because he avoided conflict with anyone who could fight back.

Dad's work isolated him by necessity, and as the years passed, he left the house on fewer and fewer occasions, often staying indoors for weeks at a time. During these times his volatility was at its greatest. The presence of another person interfered with the imaginary realities he constructed twelve hours a day. He ate supper with the family, then returned to his office, venturing downstairs when we went to bed. In the morning he rose after we left for school. He created a solitary existence through avoidance.

The nearest bathroom to my attic bedroom was across the hall from his office. One afternoon I quietly descended the steps to the bathroom and left the door slightly ajar, wary of banging it and disturbing Dad's work. I lifted the commode lid and leaned it quietly against the tank. My goal was to maintain a stream of urine in the middle of the toilet, following Mom's instructions to prevent it from spraying the floor. The door slammed open and bounced against the sink. Dad yelled from the doorway, his face red with anger, "Are you deliberately aiming in the center of the toilet to maximize sound and irritate me?"

I didn't say anything, recognizing a familiar verbal trap. Yes, I was deliberately aiming in the middle of the water. But no, it was not to irritate him. If I told the truth, it might get my mother in trouble. My silence infuriated Dad. He accused me of being deaf, stupid, or disrespectful, then asked which one it was. His voice reverberated around the small bathroom. I still didn't answer. I refused to look at him, because meeting his eye would only draw further wrath. Finally Dad turned away. "Don't flush it!" he yelled. After that, I began going to the woods to take care of my personal business.

The majority of Americans grow up in cities and suburbs and are afraid of the woods. Horror movies exploit this fear: the person alone in the forest, the sounds of unknown nocturnal animals, the sheer panic of being lost at night. My childhood was the opposite. The house scared me, but the woods were a source of solace and peace. Traipsing the woods alone, I learned to see and listen. I began to understand the overlapping cycles of nature, seasons clearly delineated by the gradual activity of bud and flower, falling leaves, rain and snow, mud and sun, the eager optimism of spring, and the dense heat of summer. I discovered the location of lady slipper and the silky jack-in-the-pulpit. I learned where trilliums grew, mayapples, ginseng, and wild blackberries. I taught myself to identify animal tracks. Upturned leaves, darker from proximity to the earth, indicated how recently an animal had traveled by. I knew where snakes and bobcats lived, that cardinals nested low to the ground and hawks quite high. I found the dens of fox and rabbit. Groundhog homes had a main entrance and two or three smaller back doors for escape. I envied their ability to come and go as they pleased through their clandestine exits.

I reserved my greatest admiration for rocks. Nothing could hurt them. They were hard and tough, capable of repelling all but the most fierce attack—a hammer or dynamite. I believed that rocks were sentient and alive. Rocks lay in place, slowly forming sockets in the earth, waiting patiently for the disruption of travel. Where there was one rock, there were more, and I concluded that they lived in families. When I found a lone rock, I transported it to a group. My strongest interest lay in the misfits: rocks with an embedded fossil, a tint of yellow, red, or black. I was particularly drawn to rocks with a hole that fully perforated the body. Such a violation was contrary to the essence of being a rock. I believed these would be shunned by others, and I carried them home, keeping them on a shelf with their brethren. At times I sensed their gratitude. The trees knew me, the animals accepted my presence, but the rocks genuinely liked me.

I needed to believe in the friendship of rocks because Dad often threatened to kill me in the basement. He mentioned several methods, but his favorite was hanging me by my thumbs, a fate that perplexed me. I didn't understand how anyone could die from it. To validate his threat, Dad said he'd killed our older brother, whose name was John. This made me particularly nervous, since my middle name is John. Maybe Dad had killed him before I was born, then named me for him. Or maybe it meant that I was next, since he'd killed a son already. After supper one night Dad elaborated on the murder of John, explaining that he'd cut up the body and flushed it down the toilet, which was why the commode never worked properly. To prove his point, he wrote "Hi John" on a scrap of paper, led my siblings and me to the bathroom, and flushed the note.

In retrospect, it's clear that my father was trying to be funny with the kind of joke that gets carried away until the humor is leached out and the audience is confused. I can forgive my father for a failed joke. I have made many myself. But as a young boy, I fully believed my father had killed my brother and therefore might kill me. Dad's office contained guns in plain sight. The available wall space held a broadsword, a battle-ax, several knives, a dagger, and a dirk. I often wondered which implement he'd used to dismember John.

The intensity of my multiple fears embarrassed me, but what really scared me was the concept of being a coward. As the oldest, I had the responsibility of courage, the same as taking care of my siblings or loving my father. Being afraid of my own murder taught me to live with impending mortality. I accepted fear and set it aside. I believe my father was governed by his fears, and in taking them out on those people closest to him, he taught me the folly of making my own important.

Chapter Fifteen

DAD WAS seventeen when his father died, their conflicts forever unresolved. Lacking an adult relationship with his own father, he didn't know how to proceed as his children aged. Before he began his career as a writer, he was gone many evenings, closing sales with clients who worked during the day. On the few nights he was home, we begged him to play cards and board games. He taught us poker. He invented a game in which we knocked marbles around the supper table with spoons. On poster board he drew a complicated route for a game based on race cars, dice, and cards. Dad had a vast capacity to make us laugh. We adored our father. He made our evenings fun.

When he began working full-time at home, the joyful nights after supper were fewer and fewer. As we got older and more mature, Dad remained the same. The humor slipped away from his limited repertoire of jokes. The deliberate naughtiness, such as a dice roll coming up six and calling it "sex," produced tense silence instead of laughter. Dad missed his attentive audience, but the old ways no longer worked. To an extent, we'd outgrown him. One by one we did the worst thing possible—we ignored him. I believe this hurt him deeply, in a way he didn't fully comprehend and we certainly could not fathom. In turn, he began ignoring us. Now that he was dead, I could give him the attention he always craved.

I began with the goal of assembling a full bibliography of his work. He'd never done it himself, and I was curious about the extent of his output. Opening the boxes in Mississippi released the scent of decaying mouse dung, dust, and cigarette smoke. It was the smell of Dad's office, my childhood, the house itself. I worked fourteen hours a day organizing thousands of letters and tens of thousands of novel pages.

More than five hundred manuscripts made several uneven columns on a long dining room table, reminding me of architectural ruins. The older drafts were crumbling at the edges. Carbon copies typed on onionskin tore easily. Metal paper clips left rust marks on the pages. I separated them into categories of porn, science fiction, and fantasy, then subdivided those into published and unpublished, short story and novel. Dad didn't date the first drafts, all of which were handwritten, their titles and character names shifting between revisions.

I went through the material again, slowly seeking insight, acting as a kind of literary detective. My father's earliest extant novel, written in college, was a three-hundred-page historical account of Rome called *The Sword and the Cross*. Completed in 1958, it included a preface declaring eleven years of research and writing begun as a teenager.

Dad's early output filled three metal filing cabinets comprising twenty-four feet of material. In the bottom drawer of the oldest cabinet, tucked in the very back, was a file that said "Paul." It contained several hand-drawn maps of St. Paul's journeys, Hippocrates' views on epilepsy, a long glossary of Hebrew and Greek, and a forty-one-page opening.

My father often said that Paul hated women, which motivated his founding of an anti-female, anti-sex cult that grew into Christianity. The proof was using the cross as a symbol. The Egyptian ankh symbolized sex and life—the lower portion being a man's genitalia, the upper part an open oval that represented a woman's vulva. According to Dad, the Christians took the ankh and closed the woman up to make the cross, representing the negative attitude toward sex in general and women especially.

I read the fragment, which detailed young Saul's childhood before he changed his name to Paul on the road to Damascus. In a long scene he watched his mother masturbate. Afterward, he suffered his first epileptic seizure, during which he condemned her sexual desire, focusing his anger on her breasts. The last page carried a handwritten comment from Dad's friend Robert E. Margroff, a minor science fiction writer: "I'll be most disappointed if the author is so inconsiderate as to die without finishing this!"

Supreme irony notwithstanding, I spent an hour pondering the comment, wondering why Dad never completed his historical novel about the beginning of Christianity. He eventually left the Church, sending letters to his priest and the pope. Dad insisted he was resigning so as not to be considered a lapsed Catholic, a term he resented for its implication that, once inculcated into the Church, he'd always be a member. Maybe his resignation eliminated the need to write the book. Or, as I began to suspect from reading more of his unfinished work, something deeper was at play—a thwarting of his own ambition by abandoning the material he cared most deeply about.

I asked my mother about the Paul book. She recalled Dad talking incessantly about it and doing enormous research. As to why he never finished it, she had this to say: "He was busy at work and didn't have a lot of time. Then when he started writing the sex books, he really liked it. The money was good. He had to write what would sell, you know. You needed dental work."

Several files contained correspondence between Dad, Robert E. Margroff, and Piers Anthony, who became a well-known writer of science fiction and fantasy. These names were important to me as a child because they were writers, and I knew that my father was trying to be one. In 1965, when I was seven, Piers Anthony and his wife visited for a couple of days. My family rarely received visitors, and the presence of strangers in the house was momentous. Robert E. Margroff stayed a couple of nights, too.

Ten months later, *If* magazine published "Mandroid," a story all three worked on at our house. Dad continued to collaborate with Margroff, and they published two more stories together. Within a few years the collaborations dwindled and the phone calls ceased. By then I was accustomed to Dad having had a falling-out with someone. He and my mother used that term exclusively, a "falling-out," code that meant Dad got mad and never spoke to that person again.

Once during my teenage years, I was wandering the woods when the weather chilled abruptly as a harbinger of rain. I hurried home. Dad stood in the backyard, nailing an open book to a log. He retreated to the shelter of a tree as a thunderstorm blew in, turning the sky dark, dumping a fierce rain. After the storm passed, I examined the object of destruction. I don't recall the book's title, but the author was his first writer friend, Piers Anthony.

Anthony maintains a website with an active blog, which included a post about Dad's death from July 2013.

> *Andy Offutt died, age 78. My awareness of him started faintly negatively, when he won a contest limited to college students that my college never was notified about. (The contest I entered didn't have a winner.) But later we got in touch and were friendly. We exchanged manuscripts for critiquing, and collaborated on a published story. My*

wife and I visited at his home in Kentucky for a week in the 1960s.

He got interested in the erotic market, so I went to a local store and bought some stuff and described what there was, helping him get started, and he became a successful erotic novelist. Later I got interested in that market myself, and asked his advice, and he was standoffish, implying that I was ignorant for asking. That was the problem with him; another writer described him as terminally shallow.

Once he collaborated with another writer, but objected to a change the other had made, so bawled him out in pages of text, then cut the letter into pieces and pasted them on a blank sheet in scattered order and sent that to the collaborator; he sent me the straight diatribe, with the stricture that I not forward it to the object of it. Considering that the collaboration was on a story the other had started, and that the suggestion had been reasonable, I was bemused.

So he was flawed, but basically he was a good guy and a good writer, and we were friends. And yes, his death makes me feel a chill wind down my spine, because we were so close in age.

The other writer mentioned was undoubtedly Margroff, with whom Dad collaborated on several unpublished novels. This anecdote perfectly summed up the darker side of my father: a cruel lashing out against a friend, then reveling in it with a mutual friend. This socially hostile aspect of his personality impacted his professional career. He ran through several agents and editors, invariably leaving on bad terms. At the slightest offense, he would cut people out of his life as swift and sure as an ax chop. Perhaps his level of insecurity was so intense that he could not bear closeness, or narcissism rendered him unable to tolerate anyone who didn't recognize his omnipotence. Dime-store psychology aside, the plain fact was that Dad got mad if he didn't get his way or if people contradicted him.

My mother told me he quit writing science fiction due to the constraints of physical reality. In fantasy he had greater freedom. His imagination could roam farther without restriction. Fantasy novels are only as successful as the underlying cohesive structure, and Dad devoted a great deal of effort to creating his worlds. Each manuscript contained detailed maps of imaginary lands and extensive glossaries to an unknown language. For books that included the formal use of sorcery, he made charts explaining their precise mechanics. He fabricated complex religions and provided a hierarchy of gods with their individual histories, feuds, and romantic liaisons. These documents served as reference material for his books.

My father didn't work with characters in landscape but populations in complicated systems. His mind contained planets and continents. He was creator, cartographer, scribe, historian, priest, and scholar. Living with these overlapping roles in imaginary environments led him to shun the company of other people. His fabrications needed sufficient space to flourish inside the walls of his head.

After organizing the manuscripts he had written, I divided his personal collection of pornography into the common forms: books, magazines, photographs, comic books, pamphlets, postcards, and calendars. The piles occupied three large tables. Needing more surface space, I set panels of plywood on sawhorses. A miscellaneous pile held two decks of nude playing cards, risqué cuff links, a pristine copy of *The First X-rated Coloring Book*, and an ink pen with a clear cylinder containing a plastic woman whose clothes fell off when the pen was turned upside down. Adult comic books narrated the sexual histories of Robin Hood and King Arthur. A retelling of fairy tales and nursery rhymes included Little Bo Peep finding a very friendly shepherd. Detailed illustrations explained how the Old Woman Who Lived in the Shoe came to have so many children. After climbing the beanstalk, Jack encountered the giant's wife, who proceeded to use him as a human dildo. Snow White endured the predations of all seven dwarfs.

There were so many overlapping batches that my initial system of organization became mired in subgenre. At first I saw myself as an archivist, but as the purview expanded, my role became that of a bureaucrat. I gave each item a designation and placed it among its own. Every time I thought I'd found an anomaly for a miscellaneous stack, another example would surface, compelling a fresh category. *The Bitch of Buchenwald* went with *Slaves of the Swastika*. Deserted island adventures formed their own group. Other subcategories included:

> farm porn
> cowboy porn
> Hollywood porn
> swapping and swinging
> rape and gang rape
> older woman/young man
> older man/young woman
> bestiality
> gay, straight, bisexual, and transgender
> incest
> anal and oral
> fem-dom: trampling, pegging, feminization
> satanism and witchcraft
> nuns and monks

inquisition torture

bondage: rope, leather, metal, rubber

doctors and nurses

teachers and students

salesmen and housewives

sex-crazed divorcées and naive coeds

spanking, flagellation, caning, flogging, birching

forced chastity

pony training and slave training

three-ways, four-ways, six-ways, and orgies

Asian, African-American, and various interracial

historic and modern

nannies and maids

urban and rural

holiday porn: Santa Claus's wife and the elves

fake case histories written by psychiatrists

The constant barrage of odd sexual content left me flailing with the knowledge of my father's dedication. This was *him*—what he enjoyed, what he collected, what he wrote. I was thankful for the utter absence of kiddie porn. My father's proclivities were not the worst. He only liked adult women. It was a cold comfort, like an executioner offering a condemned man an old rope so the bristles wouldn't hurt his neck.

Months passed during which I continued to work all day and into the evening seven days a week. When guests visited, I draped bedsheets over the tables to prevent accidental offense. What had begun as an attempt to assemble a bibliography of Dad's work had transformed into a compulsion to organize his entire library, hoping for insight. His holdings of porn were incredibly vast and inclusive. Something had governed the accumulation and I sought the mind behind it, the curating principles. It occurred to me that

I'd transformed to a version of my father—obsessed not with porn but with his preferences for porn.

There is a part of me, one I despise, that insists upon comparing myself to my father. Perhaps my poor self-regard is an unwelcome gift of his legacy, a fragment transferred to me. Dad wrote more books. He stayed married to one wife. He maintained a single, unflinching focus on his rebellious obsessions despite the odds against him. He wanted me to be my own man, and I suppose I am. But we are similar in many ways, chillingly similar. We work hard. We never give up. We don't suffer fools gladly. We prefer our time alone, away from people. We write and write and write.

My son called, seeking advice about how to handle a situation at his job. We talked for nearly an hour, longer than I ever talked with my father on the phone. Dad never gave advice. He didn't know how to offer counsel, only staunch opinions. The ones I remember are as follows:

> Picasso was a lousy artist and a put-on who conned the world.
> Elvis stinks.
> European movies stink.
> Marlon Brando stinks.
> Hemingway was a coward for his suicide.
> Jesus was a rabble-rouser who engineered his own destruction.
> Henry Miller changed the world.
> Artists and writers who become successful do so by fooling the world.
> Inferior people shouldn't breed.
> Genetics is far more important than environment.
> B. F. Skinner was a genius.

Hugh Hefner was a genius.

So was Ayn Rand.

Reincarnation is real.

Respect is more important than love.

Showing respect means offering fealty.

Capital punishment is not painful enough for killers.

Bad writers: Melville, Faulkner, Poe, Hawthorne, James, Lovecraft, Tolkien.

Good writers: Vardis Fisher, Stendhal, Freud, Shaw, Ellis.

De Sade's poor reputation is undeserved.

Eating fried chicken with one hand makes you look like a barbarian.

Men should not wear T-shirts beneath their clothes.

Women are inherently inferior to men.

Caucasians are superior to the other races.

Dad is superior to all Caucasian men.

Asians possess wisdom.

Sports are for physical freaks.

Religion is for intellectual weaklings.

Cleaning and cooking are women's work.

Women with large bosoms are attracted to powerful men.

The principles of feminism are not in conflict with pornography.

Women who were nursed as babies are bisexual.

Cheating at board games is fine.

Perverted is good.

For years I shared many of these beliefs, a boy copying his father. When I began questioning his authority, I reversed each of these precepts and believed in its opposite. Over time I formed my own opinions. Mainly I stopped believing in absolutes. They were necessary to Dad, a way of shoring up drastic decisions and rationalizing his obsessions. Leaving the Catholic Church created a space inside him previously filled by its dogma. Dad invented his own harsh evaluations of the world, decreeing everything either good or bad. Such binary thinking is a means of social control preferred by politicians, preachers, bigots, and tyrants. In an individual case, as with my father, it allowed him to live his life without regard for others.

Chapter Sixteen

MY FATHER published all his science fiction under his own name. The early stories placed him in the new wave of young writers changing the field by exploring social concerns such as sexuality, psychology, politics, and environmentalism. They focused on "soft" as opposed to "hard" science and often wrote from a more literary sensibility than their predecessors. This group included Harlan Ellison, Ursula K. Le Guin, Samuel R. Delany, and J. G. Ballard. In 1967, *If* magazine published Dad's story "Population Implosion." Its inclusion in the anthology *World's Best Science Fiction* led to an invitation to attend the World Science Fiction Convention of 1969.

My parents packed the car, left my siblings and me in the care of college students, and drove to St. Louis. Dad clipped on a name tag proclaiming him a "Pro Writer." In the elevator on the way to their hotel room, my parents met an older man wearing rumpled clothing: A. E. van Vogt, a writer Dad revered. Sincere and down-to-earth, he glanced at my father's name tag and said he'd read "Population Implosion" and admired it a great deal. This was exhilarating for a deeply insecure man whose greatest fear was being recognized for what he was—a country boy come to town—a fear shared by all rural people, and one I know very well.

In St. Louis strangers asked for his autograph. Women flirted openly. None of the men wore ties, and Dad left his in the hotel room. He met other writers with long hair and beards. Surrounded by the outrageous styles of the hippies, Mom no longer worried that the wives of doctors and professors might judge her clothing.

My parents went to St. Louis with the confidence of people who were naive to their own naïveté, and returned astonished. They had never questioned the lives they led or the motivations for their decisions; they merely followed the patterns of the time. They hated Communists, loved JFK, and flew the flag on national holidays. A gigantic Douay-Rheims Bible sat on a dais in the dining room. The goal of life was to make money and children.

A photograph from Worldcon 1969 shows my father in a gray pin-striped suit coat and a white turtleneck sweater. One arm is folded across his chest, the other propped before him, his empty hand posed as if holding an invisible object. His expression is unusual for its frowning discomfort, eyes staring upward. Dad's hair is quite short and he is clean-shaven. My mother faces him in a sleeveless cocktail dress, her hair in a perm that puffs around her head. Both appear ill at ease.

Ten months later, photographed at their next SF convention in 1970, my parents have undergone a drastic change. Around their necks are silk kerchiefs loosely held by metal clasps. Both wear rock-star sunglasses. Dad has a full beard and long hair. He's dressed in blue jeans, a thick leather belt, and a loose shirt with epaulets and flap pockets. Mom's hair is cropped into a pixie cut. She wears a blouse, jeans, and sandals. Each has a broad smile, their bodies in open, relaxed postures. Starved for a sense of social belonging, my parents had found a community that embraced them—science fiction fandom.

Local people occasionally commented that Dad was turning into a hippie, eliciting one of his many pre-thought responses: "Hippies don't shave. I'm raising a beard." Mom's new haircut alarmed me. In the Bible Belt of eastern Kentucky, I was taught at school that a woman's hair was her glory and she should never cut it off. No other woman in Haldeman wore her hair short.

The Bible vanished from the dining room, replaced by an equally large copy of *Webster's Unabridged Dictionary.* Dad gave our property the official address of The Funny Farm, putting it on legal documents, stationery, and bank checks. Entering the public world of science fiction fandom offered Dad a chance to leave identity behind—as a businessman, family man, and dutiful citizen.

For decades American literary circles ignored science fiction, placing it at the very bottom of the popular genres. This gave the writers a great deal of freedom, which they used to explore sexual themes in a more overt fashion than other books could. The science fiction market had dried up as pornography ignited, and many writers moved to porn. Among science fiction fans, there was no stigma attached to writing porn. As a result, Dad's pornography was accepted, and John Cleve transformed to a fully formed role he could embody.

From his papers I learned that Dad's experiments with a literary mask had begun at age fourteen, when he baled hay for fifty cents an hour and bought a pulp magazine featuring Sheena, Queen of the Jungle. He wrote two Sheena stories and submitted them without success under the name Anson J. O'Rourke, utilizing his initials. In childhood he was known as Jay, Little Andy, and A.J., which instilled in him the malleability of identity.

During college he wrote stories as Morris Kenniston, later choosing the name for the protagonist of his novel *The Messenger of Zhuvastou*. He used fiction to shape identity through the invention of characters, then applied the habit to his own life. Pen names provided partitions to various rooms in the mansion of his mind. Due to his habit of playacting as a child, his father called him "Lord Barrymore," after the actor. Dad's sister told me he occupied so many roles with such fervor that his true self gradually disappeared, and in later years she didn't know him anymore. He became whoever and whatever he believed himself to be at the moment—father, husband, salesman, neighbor, or John Cleve.

As Dad told me, he preferred being a big fish in a small pond: the president of his college fraternity, the only educated man in Haldeman, the top salesman in eastern Kentucky. The professional world of science fiction offered a similar limitation of scope. In 1970 and 1972, Dad published two science fiction novels, both serious examinations of near-future America. His stated goals were simple—he wanted to change the world by warning citizens of a violent and corrupt future. *Evil Is Live Spelled Backwards* is set in America under a Christian-based government with a heavily armed police force. Law enforcement seeks couples in the act of illegal sexual congress. If caught, the man is summarily executed. After sterilization, the woman becomes a prostitute for corrupt government officials. A reluctant member of the Federal Obscenity Police leads a revolution.

The protagonist of *The Castle Keeps* is a writer named Jeff Andrews who lives with his family in the house in which I grew up, on the same hill and dirt road. The interpersonal family dynamic was equally familiar—an autocratic man who demanded obedience and swift apology from his wife and kids. Here the similarities ended, and my father imagined our country's bleak future—unsanitary water and crops poisoned by pesticides. Police officers wear body armor and carry heavy arms with which they attack citizens. The world is running out of resources, particularly oil. Jeff Andrews grows a garden, stockpiles arms and food, and homeschools his children.

I read *The Castle Keeps* at age fourteen. My father asked if I'd noticed the first and last words of the book, "Dad" and "home." He told me he'd written them on purpose—for me. The protagonist's son leaves rural Kentucky for the big city, where he works as a truck driver and begins to write fiction. I never planned to follow in my father's footsteps, nor did I seek to fulfill the prophecy of his novel's characters. Nevertheless, at age nineteen, I left Kentucky for New York City, where I got a job as a truck driver. I wanted to be an actor but instead began writing fiction seriously.

Both of these early novels garnered fleeting attention and quickly went out of print. Dad was extremely disappointed with the reception, blaming the cover art and inadequate promotion. He expressed a bitter belief that years of research and revision had failed to provide a strong reward, financial or critical. Though Dad believed his social commentary had come to nothing, *The Castle Keeps* and *Evil Is Live Spelled Backwards* are his best-written books. Together they anticipated the post-9/11 militarization of local police, the rise of anti-government militias in rural areas, corporate influence on federal policy, the creation of the Tea Party, and the rightward shift of the Supreme Court.

These books, along with a handful of short stories, established my father's credentials and earned him entry to the Science Fiction Writers of America. The SFWA was a nearly ungovernable organization of misfits, rebels, and contrarians known for petty grievances and brutally absurd political maneuvering. Dad served as treasurer, then became president for two years. Lumped in with science fiction was the genre of fantasy, typified by wizards, swordplay, and gods who walked the earth. Dad moved swiftly into that field, eventually publishing twenty-four novels and editing five anthologies.

My father's parallel careers in fantasy, science fiction, and porn occurred during the same years my parents attended SF conventions—or cons—as many as nine per year, where they developed deep relationships with people they rarely saw. To the accepting world of fandom, Dad revealed his secret identity. SF fans enjoyed his porn, or at least knowing about it, and Dad savored the attention. It gave him extra cachet, a touch of glamour in the world of spacecraft and hard SF. There was a precedent of crossover between writers of porn and science fiction, but Dad was the first to forge dual careers. The con committee invited Andrew J. Offutt and got John Cleve in the bargain. He enjoyed playing both roles. At cons he'd wear one set of clothes for a science fiction panel, then change into John Cleve attire for parties. He switched name tags so often that a fan presented him with a large handmade tag of bright fabric. Stitched on one side was OFFUTT. The reverse said CLEVE.

To save money, my parents ceased hiring people to stay with us. At age twelve, I was placed in charge when they went to cons. My brother was nine, and my sisters were eight and seven. My instructions were simple: feed my siblings, feed the dogs, don't run in the house, and above all, don't tell anyone that Mom and Dad are gone. At night, I fixed supper and put my siblings to bed, reassuring them that everything was fine. After they were asleep, I sat alone in the house and fretted. I was afraid my parents would never return. I worried how we'd get food and what would happen if the electricity went out during a storm. I feared I'd lose my siblings, that I would fail at taking care of them.

Occasionally my parents were late returning on Sunday afternoon, and I called the state police to ask if there had been any fatal accidents on the interstate. Fortunately, our parents always came home. My relief was mixed with trepidation: They were exhausted, and Dad might fly off the handle at any moment. Mom slipped silently about the house, as fearful of his potential rage as we were. Many years later I understood the dire position she was in, caught between two opposing forces. Any display of loyalty to her children risked Dad's perception that she was disloyal to him, the worst act of treachery. She strode a rigid and terrible middle ground but invariably chose Dad. It was the wiser decision. His anger at her would quickly extend to all of us and last longer.

In 1971 Dad was invited to be guest of honor at a convention in Champaign-Urbana, Illinois, over Thanksgiving weekend. To offset missing the holiday, the chairman offered a free room for the Offutt kids. I had just turned thirteen. It was my first con, representing entrance to the secret world my parents inhabited. After a seven-hour drive, we arrived at dusk, underdressed for the harsh November wind cutting across the plains. Meals hadn't been part of Dad's negotiations. While everyone ate turkey at the banquet, my siblings and I shared Kraft cheese sandwiches in our room. The con had severe fiscal problems, prompting my father to forgo the final payment of his fee, which led to his being guest of honor for the next thirty years. As a result of his generosity to strangers, we never had another family Thanksgiving.

For a few years my siblings and I attended nearby cons with our parents, the only form of family vacation we ever had. Cons exposed me to an exotic world beyond the hills. Men in Haldeman carried pistols. At cons, adults wore wizard robes, swords, and space guns. I once witnessed a fatigued con chairman trying to explain to the hotel manager why a man in a *Star Trek* outfit was sitting in the kiddie pool with a woman wearing a diaphanous gown and holding a snake. Attendees tended to interact with a defensiveness born of insecurity, often dueling via their knowledge of science fiction. Some devoted their time to playing poker, bridge, and hearts. I spent an hour watching two obese fans reading side by side in the hotel lobby. Each time they turned a page, they simultaneously dipped a hand into a bag of potato chips, as if the two actions were synchronized. I understood that this was how they behaved at home, and that cons offered an opportunity to safely display their private quirks. My parents' devotion to this world confused me. I regarded fans as strange, sad, and extremely obnoxious. The violent world of Haldeman was more secure.

At cons, my siblings and I shared a hotel room with two coolers of food. We were each given a room key, cautioned against embarrassing our parents, and turned loose. They didn't tell us their room number. If we needed them for a serious reason, we were instructed to go to the main con suite and tell someone. Kids were rare at cons and there was no formal child care. My brother believed that people felt sorry for us, and my sisters retained few memories beyond a general boredom. For me, cons were an opportunity to utterly abdicate my big-brother role. Immediately upon arriving, I'd explore the hotel and memorize its layout in order to elude authority and siblings.

Aside from big-city art theaters, the only way to see vintage SF movies was at a con, an experience I couldn't bear. Fans had watched the movies so often that they competed by making loud comments intended as humorous, thereby ruining the films for anyone else. I preferred an area called the Huckster Room, set aside for dealers in books, magazines, comic books, original art, and posters. Already an avid comic collector, I saw cons as a way to improve my holdings. My brother and I shared an old leather suitcase with a hinged flap that separated the two sides. He filled his half with clothes and extra underwear. I stocked my section with comics to swap, and wore the same outfit the entire time. Now and then I caught an untoward glimpse of the politics of fandom—hucksters who didn't like my father drove me off with rude comments.

At the time I didn't know I was at the forefront of what would become a massively popular "geek culture" as cons splintered into subgroups, evolving to widespread acceptance. Comic Con currently draws over 150,000 attendees. The Society for Creative Anachronism has its own formal gatherings, as do *Star Trek,* anime, pulps, fantasy, cyberpunk, steam punk, alternate history, and gaming. In the early 1970s, they were all huddled beneath the ragged tent of SF cons, which doubled as sexual free-for-alls. Mom and Dad lodged themselves on a separate floor from us. They shared two rooms with a linking door. Years later my father told me it was a means to accommodate private liaisons on both their parts.

My mother's seamless veneer of politesse was unusual among fans, whose interpersonal skills were on a par with those of chess players and degenerate gamblers. Fans revered my father as royalty, granting him constant attention. They gave him swords and daggers, homemade chain mail, whips and leather cuffs, bottle after bottle of bourbon, plaques, statues, and original art. Dad was charismatic and funny until someone failed to grant the proper respect, usually by having the audacity to speak. Dad then subjected that person to a public humiliation that made others uncomfortable, an interaction that enhanced my father's notoriety. I learned to avoid Dad, who gave me dirty looks and deliberately turned his back if I didn't vacate the area quickly. It was similar to our home life, except the hotel offered an alternative to the woods as refuge.

My parents cultivated a special con wardrobe. Dad dressed in dashikis or open-necked shirts with giant collars, zipper boots, wide leather belts, and flared pants. Mom wore short skirts and low-cut blouses that zipped up the front with no bra, high boots, and tight belts. John Cleve wore a long djellaba with nothing underneath, while Mom wore a floor-length polyester gown. To complement Dad's leather-and-denim leisure suit, Mom had a leather miniskirt. My parents were a compelling pair, and I was awestruck by the figures they cut. Though they ignored me at cons, I never loved them more, drawn to the personas they'd crafted for public consumption.

As with any subculture, a particular argot developed, insider talk that marked familiarity and experience on the part of the speakers. The vocabulary served a purpose similar to Cockney rhyming slang and the Irish travelers' *shelta,* cryptolects that excluded strangers. The lingo of fandom enjoyed puns, acronyms, deep insider jokes, and the unusual habit of adding the letter "h" to words in order to make them more "fhannish." Fan slang was molten, shifting from verb to noun to modifier at will, used orally and in print.

In the cleverly agile minds of SF fans, the word "fan" underwent many permutations, including pluralizing it to "fen." Newcomers were "neo-fen." The word "fannish" was used as a compliment, "unfannish" as a pejorative. The language itself was called "fanspeak," and included "corflu," an abbreviation for the correction fluid used when typing fanzines; "filking," which referred to the playing and singing of songs; and "LoC," which meant "letter of comment" to a fanzine and begat "locced" and "loccer."

Eager to fit in, I learned fanspeak rapidly, becoming well versed in this clandestine coded language, unknown in the hills. Like my parents, I had no one with whom to share it. Unlike them, I didn't crave further contact with speakers of the cant.

In late June 1972, my family undertook a two-week trip that encompassed three cons. We loaded the Mercedes on a Friday. Mom and Dad shared the driving while the four of us kids sprawled in the backseat, feet propped on coolers, our luggage in the trunk. We drove to Cincinnati for MidwestCon, a boring event due to its deliberate lack of programming. After three days, we embarked on the second leg. Somewhere in rural Indiana, the Mercedes began emitting a loud and steady sound of rasping metal, and we heard an explosion from under the hood. The engine immediately stalled. Dad steered to the shoulder. Frustrated and furious, he put me to work gathering pieces of the engine scattered along the road behind us. I pulled my T-shirt away from my body to form a basket for the chunks of metal, which burned my fingers. A state trooper arranged for a tow to a garage, where we remained for several hours.

According to the mechanic, a red oil light on the dashboard indicated that the car had run completely out of oil. The Mercedes had thrown a rod, meaning a piston had broken free of the crankshaft and exploded through the bottom of the engine block. Obtaining the necessary replacement parts would be delayed due to the Fourth of July weekend. Many phone calls later, fans going to the same con stopped and gave us rides, splitting up the family. My brother and I joined a strange pair of men, unkempt and smelly, who argued nonstop about *Silent Running*. We arrived in Wilmot, Wisconsin, tired, hungry, and forlorn. Dad was angry at Mom for not noticing the oil light. My brother and I were scared from the erratic driving of the *Silent Running* freaks. My sisters were withdrawn and silent.

WilCon was an invitation-only affair held at a family-owned ski resort with a fake mountain. The lodge was closed in summer, and people slept on cots, furniture, the floor, the porch, and in dozens of tents. Mom and Dad shared the bedroom of the hosts. My siblings and I joined two other kids in the basement, lined up in sleeping bags. WilCon was not really a con at all but a constant party that had evolved from a one-day picnic to a four-day gathering of fans and hippies. In fannish circles, it was well known for its exclusivity. Various legends had accrued: A *Star Trek* actor buried treasure on the property; an adored fan dropped dead one year; another fan repeatedly ran into trees while chasing a Frisbee under the influence of hallucinogenics. Couples swapped mates, swapped again, and kept swapping.

Loud rock music began playing early in the morning and continued late into the night. Meals were less than savory, prepared by a rotating crew of forced volunteers. All day long, people played cards, washed dishes, and debated the influence of E. E. "Doc" Smith on the novels of Robert Heinlein. They also consumed enormous quantities of alcohol. The scent of marijuana wafted from the only closed door in the house. I didn't like the taste of alcohol, but the smell of pot enticed me to the dope room, where I stood outside the door taking great inhalations and wondering if I was high enough to run into a tree.

Ever observant and in constant motion, I drifted the grounds like a coyote, circling the periphery, then moving in for a closer look. Nude people flashed skin through open tent flaps or skinny-dipped in the nearby pond. My mother checked on my siblings and me a few times a day, mainly at meals and in the late evening. I never interacted with my father, who pointedly ignored me, perpetually surrounded by sycophants.

One afternoon the six of us kids walked to the pond to swim. At fourteen, I was the oldest. The dark water was topped in places by a green scum. Occasionally a fish brushed my legs. With no hills to block my view, I could see farther than at home, the pond an oasis beneath a broad expanse of deep blue sky. I stood in the cool water, watching the surface ripple away from my body in fading rings of sunlight and shadow. I began moving my hands in the water to see what happened when the ripples overlapped. Someone threw a rock that struck me in the head. I immediately fell.

I regained consciousness beneath the surface of the pond and rose, disoriented and dazed, spitting water and choking. My sisters began screaming. My brother ran to the house. I stumbled out of the pond and staggered across the field. Adults found me wandering alone, a deep gash in the hairline above my left eye, limping from a thorn in my bare foot. Blood streamed down my torso and legs. Someone took me to the hospital in town, where a doctor shaved a patch of hair around the wound and stitched it shut. I returned to the con under sedation, embarrassed at the situation. For the next two days I overheard my father repeating the same words again and again: "The doctor was a square. Look how much hair he shaved off!" I realized that impressing the hippies with his use of slang mattered more to him than my health.

We got a ride to Indiana, where the Mercedes had been repaired, and drove to Peoria, Illinois, for PeCon. My head hurt constantly. The bandages weren't changed often enough and the wound began seeping. Each morning I awoke with my head stuck to the pillow. I remained in the hotel room, watching television and taking aspirin. My siblings stayed with me, our family roles reversed as they took care of their older brother, preparing meals of cheese and crackers, peanut butter, and fruit. They gave me pillows and changed the channels on the TV. For those three days, despite my persistent headache and cloudy vision, I felt protected and cared for.

We returned to Haldeman, where I recovered amid the woods I loved, grateful for the familiar culture. One neighbor plowed by mule. Another man nailed dead squirrels upside down to a tree in front of his house and gutted them, allowing the entrails to fall to the ground. He peeled off the skin and carried the carcasses inside to cook. The furry hides remained on the tree, turning black with rot, flapping in the wind. The stew he made tasted better than anything at a con, especially with a glass of well water cold enough to numb my gums.

But I had seen another world, exotic and strange, and at times I missed it. I grew my hair long to be more like fans. If I looked like them, my parents might have more interest in me.

Chapter Seventeen

IN THE strict hierarchy of the hills, people from Morehead were at the top of the heap. Next came families who lived on the outskirts, then those with homes along the few blacktop roads that headed into town. Last were country people like myself. Social strata was based on geography and family name. Both of mine were suspect. These distinctions became clearly delineated when I attended Rowan County High School, ten miles away in Morehead.

I loved the boys and girls I'd grown up with. Fourteen of us had moved through the Haldeman grade school together, but now we were dispersed among the largest entering freshman class in the high school's history. We lost our sense of belonging. One by one, many of my classmates abandoned the routine of attending school. Dropping out was not expected but was accepted and of minimal concern. At four feet, eleven inches tall, I was the shortest kid with the longest hair, allegedly the smartest. As my childhood friends left school, I became socially isolated.

My parents were friends with the head of the theater program at the local college, and when a play called for a child actor, I was added to the cast and performed in several productions. Teachers viewed this as a promising development and excused me from school to attend rehearsals. I swiftly took advantage of the circumstances. My daily pattern was to ride the bus to school, check in to morning homeroom for attendance, leave school under the guise of "play practice at the college," and catch the bus home in the afternoon. I began keeping my bicycle in town and often arranged to sleep at various people's homes—friends of my parents or college students to whom I had become a kind of theater mascot.

By the time I was fifteen, my family was accustomed to my absences—wandering the woods, eating elsewhere, sleeping in town. What mattered to my parents were academic grades. The night before an exam, I stayed home and read the textbook, then aced the test. Of equal importance were granting utter obedience to Dad and never causing my mother public embarrassment. With this patina of civility thus attended to, I was free, and Morehead was mine to explore.

I don't remember how I met the fatman. I assume he approached me. He lived in town on the second floor of a small building, where he rented a single room with a bathroom in the hall. He was nice to me, buying me candy bars and bottles of pop, which my parents never allowed me to have. I told him about my life and the girls I liked. The fatman listened to me. He offered a form of sympathy and attentiveness that I needed. He accepted that I wanted to be an actor or a comic book artist, and he believed such aspirations weren't ridiculous. He didn't talk about himself but implied that he'd experienced life beyond the confines of Rowan County, and that I would like it out there when I finally left.

The fatman's room was small, with no chair, and we both had to sit on the bed. He suggested I lie on my back, and the whole time

I pretended it was happening to someone else. I don't remember his name or what he looked like. I don't recall the print on the wallpaper or the color of the bedspread. What I do remember is the overhead light fixture, a plain globe in a ceramic setting that emitted a dim yellowish light. Surrounding the globe and painted over many times were plaster rosettes with narrow leaves. I remember the light because I spent all my time staring at it and waiting until I could leave.

Afterward, the fatman said he liked me and gave me money. I left the room and walked to the drugstore, where my mother picked me up after shopping for groceries. I bought a lot of comics at the drugstore. Mom didn't ask where I got the money.

When I returned to his room a week later, I climbed the steps very slowly, trying not to make any noise because I didn't want to get the fatman in trouble. A clot of tension rose along my spine, vibrating like an embedded blade. I felt hollow—my heart pounding, sweat trickling down my sides, my mouth dry, my stomach congealed to stone. The fatman opened the door and ushered me in. The bed sagged when he sat on it. The money lay in sight on the bedside table. Time stopped as I slid away from my body, imagining a life beyond the hills. I would be a movie actor. Beautiful women would throw themselves at me. I was the mayor's son, the governor's nephew. I was secretly adopted. I was anyone but a lonely kid feeling the dampness of fat fingers in my pants.

Later I decided that my parents would be proud of my open-mindedness in such a small town. They considered themselves progressive. I believed that what I was doing with the fatman made me similar to them. They wrote porn and had affairs. If they knew about the fatman, they would respect me, maybe even like me.

The fatman took me to the movies. We stood in line but didn't have to buy tickets. The fatman looked at the owner, put his hand on my shoulder, and nodded once. The owner stared at me without changing expression and let us in free. The fatman bought me a large buttered popcorn. Occasionally Mom made popcorn at home, but she never put butter on it. I felt special, eating buttered popcorn and watching *The Godfather,* which affected me in a very powerful way. I'd never seen a movie that long or that slow. The world it depicted was utterly foreign, but I understood its insular nature, the power dynamics, the violence and loyalties. After the movie, the fatman gave me a dime because I insisted on calling my father and telling him that if anything ever happened to him, I would avenge his death. I was crying into the phone. My father said little. I could hear the clatter of his typewriter keys as I spoke.

The fatman wanted me to touch him in his bed, but I refused. I explained that I liked girls, although I'd never been with one. I'd kissed three and touched one's bra strap. The fatman offered me two hundred dollars to help him make a movie. They'd shoot the whole thing in a hotel room nearby, but I'd have to touch a man, maybe another boy about my age. I told him that I really wanted to be with a girl and suggested we make that kind of movie instead. He said if I made a movie with a man, he would provide me with a girl afterward. I told him no. He told me to think about it, but I didn't. I looked at the light fixture and went away in my mind.

I'd developed the ability to go rapidly, to vanish from circumstances and enter a trancelike state in which I was a prince with a personal garrison at my command, a lavish kingdom to rule, and a harem of lovely women. Abruptly I was back in the dim room. My legs were bare and cold, my body tense. The fatman was breathing hard. I took the money and left.

The last time I went to the room, I encountered another boy on the steps. He was a year older than I was, with long hair the same color as mine. New to school, he lived with his mother in a trailer. I'd seen him outside the building before, but we both pretended we hadn't noticed the other. This time he was crouching on the steps. He motioned me to be quiet. I joined him, moving silently. We were midway up the staircase. The bathroom was at the top of the steps and the door was partly open. Through it we could see the fatman standing in the shower, his vast naked bulk exposed. He was vomiting and defecating simultaneously. It was a sickening sight, so repulsive that it was hard to stop staring. The fatman began crying, an uncontrollable sobbing that made his shoulders quake, his torso ripple. He leaned on the wall as if in surrender.

The other boy and I slipped down the stairs and laughed about what we'd seen. What else could we do? We laughed at the hideous sight. We never talked about it and he soon quit school. A few years passed before I wondered if he'd made a movie at the motel. By then he was already dead of an overdose. The fatman once suggested I bring my brother to visit, and I got very angry. The only good that I can find in all this now is that I protected my brother. At least I did that.

The fatman left town as suddenly as he'd appeared, and I didn't speak to anyone about him. Instead, I began to shoplift. Every time I entered a store, I walked around as if browsing, while secretly examining lines of sight and avenues of getaway. I was a meticulous planner. The best technique was to set the object I intended to steal near the door, then buy something cheap that required a shopping bag. On my way out of the store, I'd surreptitiously slip the preset goods into the bag. I got very scared as I walked to the door, my body encased in the same adrenalized state as when climbing the steps to the fatman's room. I breathed slowly through my mouth, sweating inside my clothes. On the sidewalk outside, I felt the euphoria of relief at having gotten away. Stealing made me feel bad about myself, but that didn't matter, because feeling bad was my normal state. I never got caught. I never stole anything I really wanted.

In a college psychology class, I read an article that referred to people who'd been sexually abused as "victims." This made me uneasy because I didn't like the idea of being a victim. I knew the whole fatman business was my fault. Nobody had forced me to enter that building and climb those stairs and push open the dark wooden door. I'd gone there freely. I'd been there more than once. I felt special. I felt bad. I wondered if I was gay. I dropped the class and got stoned, then drunk, and stayed that way for a good while.

Twenty-five years later I began talking about the fatman. I thought I might feel relieved or unburdened, but I didn't. I told my wife. I told my parents and siblings in a group letter, which I suppose was cowardly, perhaps even cruel. It was shocking enough that no one knew how to respond. My father, surprisingly, called. He wanted to know if the fatman still lived in the county. Coincidentally, Dad evoked *The Godfather,* saying that he would send Vito and Luigi to kill the man. I didn't tell him how that particular movie had figured in to things so long ago.

After revealing my old secret, I mainly felt embarrassed. Worse things happened to other boys, and much worse things happened to women. I was never forced or hurt. It was a long time ago. I knew that I should find it in myself to forgive the fatman, an act that ultimately would benefit me. But I couldn't do it. I'd spent too many years hoping he went to prison. I hoped every inmate spat on him in the corridors. I wanted them to fill his food with poison, smack him around in the yard, and ambush him in the shower. I wanted him to be scared and alone. I wanted his life to be so miserable that he spent every day wishing he were someone else. I wanted him to memorize the dim flat light fixture in his cell. I wanted him as dead as I felt, as dead as I still feel sometimes, as dead as the other boy I saw on the steps will always be.

Chapter Eighteen

WHEN I was fifteen, the most direct impact of my experience with the fatman was a deep fear that I was secretly gay. The answer to that was obvious—find a girl who'd let me have sex with her—but I couldn't get dates, let alone sex. Before my father shut down his insurance agency, he'd accidentally given his secretary a porn manuscript to type. Rumor and gossip about my father's writing spread through the county. Though tame by pornographic standards, his SF novels contained descriptions of sex that offended local people. As a result, concerned parents refused to let their daughters go out with me.

Dad never talked about his work overtly; the formal subject was forbidden, but I knew about it and sought the porn when my parents were away. I was as afraid of the material as I was intrigued. That it was secret made it "bad," which increased its appeal. I wondered if my mother knew about it, then realized she had to—she did his typing.

Spanking figured prominently in most of the books. It was appealing in the abstract, since it seemed to induce sex, but being beaten by grade school teachers had left me with a disregard for pain and punishment.

The books were detailed and graphic but lacked warmth. Sex took place for its own sake, often part of a fierce power dynamic. Porn supplied me with an understanding of the mechanics of sex—anatomy, technique, timing, and aftermath—but no sense of intimacy. Women were fiercely resistant until forced into accepting their buried desire, whereupon they became compliant and willing. On the other hand, my experience with the fatman made me absolutely determined never to coerce another person into a vulnerable situation. These two attitudes conflicted. The result was extreme trepidation, beneath which lay the burning curiosity of all teenagers.

It never occurred to me that young women were just as interested in sex as I was. My assumption, based on porn and the conservative culture of the hills, was that females were essentially asexual. They had to be tricked into sex, or married. I didn't want to participate in either scenario. Boys were prone to bragging about their sexual prowess, and I naively believed the lies I heard at school. It seemed as if everyone except me was having secret fun. Like most teenagers, I felt I had nowhere to turn, no one to trust.

I began spying on a hippie commune in a narrow holler, occasionally glimpsing a woman with no shirt. The hills offered free clay for potters, cheap rent in general, a gorgeous landscape, and soil that was highly suitable to the cultivation of marijuana. The current wave of visitors came from northern cities and spoke with heavy accents. Many were rich kids slumming, as if visiting Appalachia was a tour of duty necessary to acquire their countercultural bona fides back home. They arrived for brief periods and left. The old folks called them "hemorrhoids," saying the good ones came down and went back up, but the bad ones came down and stayed. People left them alone.

After weeks of clandestinely watching the commune, I decided to steal their marijuana, then trade it back to them for sex. A buddy and I made a night mission, moving furtively along a ridge behind the hippie house and down through the woods. We used our pocketknives to cut the plant at the base and escaped into the shadows. The marijuana was more of a bush, and we didn't know what to do with it.

In an abandoned smokehouse, we built a small fire and heated some leaves, which ignited. We began inhaling the acrid smoke and lay around pretending to be high, not really knowing the effects but making lofty claims—we could fly, see through walls, become invisible. Finally we admitted that the only results were seared throats and throbbing headaches. We concluded it had to be cured like tobacco, and I hatched a plan even more absurd than trading dope for sex.

We carefully stripped the leaves and packed them in four bread sacks, tied off the ends, and pressed them flat. We slid them under our clothes, hitchhiked to town, and went to a Laundromat. During a lull when it was empty, we dumped the marijuana into a dryer, cranked the heat to the highest setting, and stood guard. Within ten minutes the pungent scent of marijuana filled the Laundromat. We monitored the load, but the leaves hadn't changed colors to indicate a quickened rate of curing. The next time we checked, half the leaves blew into the room and scattered across the floor. My buddy and I fled.

That summer our family attended MidwestCon, which turned out to be my last con. Dad said he'd driven the Mercedes into the Ohio River, to collect insurance money, and bought a VW squareback. My youngest sister rode in the back, tucked into a small space among the luggage. The minute we arrived at the hotel, Dad began operating in full John Cleve mode, refusing to acknowledge his children. The only other teenager at the con was the fourteen-year-old daughter of a minor SF writer who also wrote porn. We talked the first night. Tessa had run away to New Orleans for a while but now lived with her father, whom she hated. He ignored her and he drank and had too many rules. I told her I knew exactly what she meant. We agreed on everything—fans were the biggest weirdos in the world, cons were boring, and our parents didn't care.

The next day I suggested we swim in the motel pool, mainly for an opportunity to see her in a bathing suit. She refused on the grounds that cons were full of old perverts, then crooked her finger in a "follow me" motion. We rode the elevator to the fifth floor, the walls of which were painted a deep shade of blue. She led me to a door with a sign that said "Housekeeping." Inside was a wall of shelves that held sheets, towels, toilet paper, plastic cups, and tiny packages of soap. Tessa unfolded a roll-away bed. The only illumination came from a wide crack beneath the door.

Prior to this, I had kissed three girls from other counties and believed I could acquit myself well, but Tessa explored my mouth like she was planning a topographical map. Her body pressed against mine, her hands were on me, and I became lost in a delirium of desire. She took off her shirt, then her pants, the dim light outlining her body. I could not believe I was actually seeing a naked girl. Tessa quickly removed my shoes, then dragged off my pants and pushed me back on the bed. I could feel the softness of her chest, the smoothness of her skin. She put her arms around me. We rolled over and I held her as tightly as possible. I frankly thought I was going to die. Nothing had ever felt better, and I wanted to prolong it until I did die.

I bucked my hips and squirmed like a salamander, trying to stay on my knees and elbows so as not to mash Tessa too much. I mainly just hoped for the best. She put one arm across my back and the other on my hip and began to assist my maneuvering.

After a while, during which I lost all sense of time, our activity slowed.

Enduring the fatman's touch had instilled in me the habit of ignoring all sensation and withholding any reaction. As a result, I was unable to climax with Tessa. However, my father's books had taught me about female anatomy to the point that I could provide her with ample pleasure several times. She started putting on her clothes, and I did, too. When we were fully dressed, she said, "You're better than guys three times your age."

"Thanks," I said.

She opened the door and we stepped into the hall, blinking against the sudden light. At the elevator I heard the sound of an opening door. Down the hall, my father stepped from a room. He said something low and a woman responded with laughter. Dad closed the door behind him and straightened his hair.

I pushed the elevator button repeatedly, fearful of getting caught. Tessa and I descended to the lobby without talking. Dazed and happy, I wanted to remain in her company, but she avoided me for the rest of the con. I didn't mind. I'd finally had sex.

Chapter Nineteen

DURING MY senior year in high school, my father and I were in perpetual conflict. Instead of talking, we avoided each other. My misery wasn't entirely his fault, but he'd taught me to blame others for my misfortune, and I dutifully blamed him. He seemed to regard every word I uttered as a challenge to him. Perhaps it was. No one else stood up to Dad. I protected my siblings, but nobody protected me. I was on my own and I knew it.

Dad was forty-two, at the height of his porn career. The house was mired in tension, seething with sexuality. John Cleve presided over everything with a tyrannical intensity. We still ate supper together, but the family scattered immediately afterward. My sisters and brother stayed in their rooms. I roamed the woods at night, fearless and hoping for trouble. A friend had an old car, nearly indestructible, unable to reach high speed. We began wrecking it on purpose for excitement.

A long argument between my father and me ended with us in separate parts of the house. Dad stomped into the room where I stood and handed me a note. I saved it for years, committing it to memory:

*Your need to have the last word makes it impossible to
talk with you. Here, then, is mine.*

The next day I took the military aptitude test. It was the first
year the ASVAB was unilaterally administered by all the services.
Each branch received the test results and competed for the top
candidates. I was inordinately proud that my score was the highest in the state. It didn't occur to me that the military test was
not that difficult and academic standards for Kentucky were not
very high.

Each branch actively recruited me. Having never seen an
airplane, I ruled out the air force. I eliminated the navy because
I didn't know how to swim. I never fully understood what the
Marine Corps did, since "marine" meant water, but they were
ground troops. I settled on the army because the recruiter told
me I could wear a short-hair wig instead of cutting my Southern-
outlaw hair. He explained that since the Vietnam War was over, I
wouldn't have to take orders if I didn't want to. I believed his lies
and enlisted.

My ASVAB scores were high enough that a different sergeant
arrived, a stern man who represented Military Intelligence. Orig-
inally from Texas, he said he'd been the same at my age, brimful
of brains with nowhere to aim them. The army, particularly intel,
helped him reach his potential. He hinted that after my service,
I'd have opportunities to work for the government in an interesting capacity. His implications and vagueness impacted me more
than the overt sales pitch from the other recruiters. I left that
meeting with a clear vision of my glorious future: paratrooper,
army intel, college on the GI Bill, then the Central Intelligence
Agency.

I'd grown up with Vietnam as just another television show and
was disappointed when the war ended before I got a chance to

fight. Watching *The Man from U.N.C.L.E.* influenced my plan to join the CIA as much as reading *Harriet the Spy* and Kipling's *Kim*. I began consuming histories of the clandestine services and espionage novels, studying them as textbooks for my future occupation. I invented secret codes and practiced the use of invisible writing with lemon juice and milk. Spies trusted no one and disregarded authority. They often came from a family in which duplicity was accepted and normal, thus easing the transition to professional skulduggery. My insecurities were an asset: I wanted to be liked. I needed to believe in something larger and more important than myself. Patriotism was as good a fit as any.

My motivation for military service was unrelated to family tradition or duty. I was reckless and young but mainly angry. I wanted to jump out of airplanes with a rifle and shoot people. I wanted to get out of Haldeman and far away from my father.

Though determined to leave, I felt like I was abandoning my siblings. I became anxious about my future letters home. I didn't want to worry them, but failing to correspond would increase their concern. I began planning countermeasures, settling on disinformation as the best strategy.

The periodical area of the Morehead library contained several years' worth of *Reader's Digest,* which had a monthly section called "Humor in Uniform," composed of anecdotes contributed by veterans. I stopped attending school and went to the library, where I read dozens of these stories. Basic training was ten weeks long, and my plan was to send two letters home per week, relating incidents from *Reader's Digest* as if they were mine. Most had the ring of truth and a lighthearted intimacy that would ease my siblings' worry. I subdivided the brief narratives into specific categories—lousy food, clothing that didn't fit, bad weather, hateful chores, and the sergeant's unreasonable anger. Within two weeks, I had compiled a notebook of humorous episodes, transcribed and organized into sections, complete with a title page that said "Letters Home."

Because I was underage, my parents needed to sign the induction papers. After supper one night, I told them my plan and presented the legal documents. There was no discussion, no suggestion of finishing high school or going to college. My mother said nothing. Dad asked if I was sure. I nodded. He signed the form with his customary and well-practiced flourish, as if inscribing a book to a fan, and left the table dramatically. Mom silently watched him go and avoided looking at me.

I'd been an honor student throughout high school, with straight A's in English, history, and science. Teachers had fawned over my intelligence since first grade, even the ones who beat me. I was a strong candidate for scholarships to top colleges around the country. But no one—not a single teacher, parent, or family friend—encouraged me to further my education. My future lay exclusively in my own ignorant hands and that of the U.S. Army.

In May the recruiter drove four of us boys to Lexington for the induction physical. We didn't talk in the car, all of us nervous, the recruiter abruptly serious. We hadn't seen this side of him. Gone was the jocular charisma, replaced by grim purpose. We joined a hundred or so other boys in a large facility the size of a gymnasium with an array of medical personnel. Metal racks covered by cloth were separated into sections for various tests. We stripped to our underwear and moved in slow lines: pulse checked, blood taken, mouth and ears examined, testicles squeezed while we coughed. We laughed our way through all of it. Occasionally an examiner culled someone out and sent him to get dressed. We looked at him with scorn—he wasn't up to snuff, no longer one of us. Those boys appeared sad, walking with their heads lowered in defeat. We speculated as to the reason: *too fat, too short, too dumb, too fucking ugly!* Our jokes concealed the lurking fear that any one of us could be next.

After a few hours I was pronounced extremely fit: good heart, vision, and hearing. My upper and lower extremities functioned with no defects. I was disease-free, with fine circulation. A doctor pulled me aside, and for the next two hours I urinated into a plastic canister again and again. I thought it was a special procedure reserved for future spies, a test of endurance, and I refused to complain or ask questions. The other boys in my group moved on, leaving me alone to supply samples. The last doctor said: "Albumin in your urine. No branch will take you." Standing in my underwear, I became so upset I began to cry, then felt humiliated for having done so. I didn't cry again for fifteen years.

During our long car ride home, the three other boys chattered and laughed and beat on each other. The recruiter regained his former cheer. He told dirty jokes and allowed us to smoke in the car. I sat against a door, face pressed to the window. I didn't see the land go by or listen to the others. Awash in despair, I felt like a failure, as if I'd let down the recruiter. Worse, I had no idea what to do. I'd already quit high school, hadn't applied to any colleges, and feared being permanently trapped in my father's house. The one act I'd taken to exert control over my life was thwarted by piss in a cup. My own body had betrayed me. I didn't even know what albumin was.

The recruiter returned to his small office in Morehead and prepared the final paperwork for the lucky boys. I walked four miles before catching a ride to the turnoff for my home hill. I climbed the quarter-mile dirt road slowly. For twelve years I'd traveled up and down the hill on foot. I knew how the light and shadows fell, where the potholes developed, the steepness of every step. I'd walked the dirt in full dark with no moon or stars, at dawn in mist and dew, during rain and snow. At a flat curve, the only place two cars could pass, I began throwing rocks in the creek. The absolute certainty of my future was obliterated. I wondered how many rocks it would take to fill the creek. I now had that sort of time. Stuck forever in Haldeman, I could build a dam, rock by rock.

Long after night arrived, I sat in the road, clearing the space around me until I was down to dust. I went home and told my parents the news. Their reaction was the same as when I'd announced my intention to enlist. They nodded and said nothing. In my bedroom I discarded my notebook of anecdotes. I rearranged the items on my shelves—a jar of wheat pennies, a box of feathers, hundreds of comic books, and lucky rocks. My brief brush with the adult world of military service made my collections seem silly, the accumulations of a child. I lay in bed unable to sleep, tense and furious. A few months later I enrolled at Morehead State University, the only college in the hills.

I've since learned that albumin is a type of protein essential to building muscle and healthy plasma. Its appearance in my urine was a onetime fluke, unexplainable, never materializing again. In 1976 the army was bloated with troops and attempting to downsize, thus increasing the rigor of its requirements. I've often wondered how my life might have unfolded with successful enlistment. Every time I meet veterans, I feel a twinge of envy. The benefits are clear to me now: a structure that provides camaraderie, meals, clothing, lodging, and training. The potential existed for a strong role model, perhaps a man of honor and integrity. I might have hated military life or never used the GI Bill. Or maybe today I'd be mingling with bureaucrats in D.C.'s Beltway, commuting daily to Langley, working as a senior analyst. Or perhaps like the other boys with whom I enlisted, I'd have been discharged quickly, returning home with a deeper understanding of personal defeat.

Chapter Twenty

MOM HAD lived her entire life in two counties of Kentucky. She'd never lived alone. Three months after Dad's death, the movers transported her possessions to her new home in Mississippi, a few blocks from the Oxford square. For the first time in her life, she was autonomous. Mom promptly bought a new bed and hung her favorite pictures. I'd never seen her so happy. She could sleep as late as she wanted, eat a roast beef sandwich for breakfast, and read in bed. The only rules were hers. She applied for a passport. In the ensuing year, she traveled to Germany, Spain, London, Paris, Prague, California, Texas, and Virginia.

My own house was seven miles away, in the country. After thirty-five years, our situations had reversed: Mom lived in town and I had returned to a rural environment. I saw her at least once a week, usually for a meal or a local literary event. Mom was socially adventurous, liked to laugh, and preferred her cocktails promptly at six P.M. As her young neighbors said: "Miss Jodie's cool." We looked forward to our time together. Our conversations were very open and honest. Now that Dad was dead and Mom no longer lived in Rowan County, she felt comfortable discussing pornography.

At times I worried about her reaction to my writing a book about Dad and my childhood. Ten years before, Dad had called me with express orders not to write about his career as a pornographer, a project he'd learned I was working on from a magazine. I explained that porn didn't have the same negative connotation that it once had. He didn't believe me and I appealed to his vanity, suggesting I interview John Cleve for the book. Dad's voice took on a slightly mournful tone. "That won't work," he said. "Ol' John's clothes don't fit anymore. He's gone, son. He's gone."

A week later Mom made a rare visit to my house and asked me to abandon the book I'd begun. Surprised and irritated, I pointed out that since she and Dad had mass-produced porn without consulting their kids, I should have the same literary freedom as an adult. Mom said they'd been very careful to keep their lives separate—the wild excesses of fandom and the more sedate life in Haldeman.

"There was no overlap," she said.

"There was an overlap," I said. "Your kids. We were the overlap."

She nodded, then told me her own objection. She didn't think too many people in Morehead would actually read my book, but they'd know about it from the Lexington paper and naively confuse pornography with smut or dirty books. This surprised me, and I asked what porn was if it wasn't smut or dirty books.

"Sex guides," she said. "For couples."

"Most people wouldn't see a difference," I said.

"Your father did."

I didn't say anything because the language sounded more like Dad's than hers. Finally she gave me the real reason—she was afraid the women in her Weight Watchers group would hear about the porn and ask her to leave the meetings. She'd lost fifteen pounds and felt good about herself. I didn't say anything. I was trying to comprehend Mom's situation. It wasn't about her weight, it was her fear of social rejection. She had lived most of her life with a difficult man. Mom was like a trusty in a prison, unable to leave but receiving special privileges for service and good behavior. Her kids could escape but not her. Out of deference to my mother, I set the project aside.

Recently over lunch in Mississippi, she mentioned that Dad had given his own mother a copy of *Mongol!*, his twelfth book. I expressed surprise, since it was a John Cleve novel. Mom explained that Dad used index cards and rubber bands to block off the sex chapters and prevent his mother from reading them. I nodded, remembering Dad telling me that the loincloth worn by primitive people simultaneously protected the genitals and called attention to them. Partitioning the porn was a way of pointing it out.

Dad often said that *Mongol!* was John Cleve's best book. I had never read it, never even seen a copy, but I remembered his excitement about the research. I was nine when he explained that the invention of the stirrup revolutionized war, allowing men to fight efficiently on horseback. My father stood with his legs spread wide as if astride a horse, bouncing on his toes to demonstrate how mounted archers used their knees as shock absorbers against the jolting gait of their mounts. Genghis Khan's men hated to leave the saddle. If a horse was exhausted from a hard ride, the soldier cut a vein in its neck, drank its blood until the horse faltered, then lithely switched to another steed mid-gallop. Under Dad's enthusiastic tutelage, I considered Genghis Khan a romantic and mythical hero on a par with King Arthur and Robin Hood. Years later I learned that approximately sixteen billion humans carry DNA from Genghis Khan due to his custom of raping women.

After the conversation with my mother, I went home and located a copy of *Mongol!* in one of the many cardboard boxes.

Published by Brandon House in 1970, its olive-green cover depicted a prancing satyr beneath the title, large white letters in a quasi-Asian design.

John Cleve's
MONGOL!

I admired the emphasis on the author's name, as if John Cleve were a known entity and the reading public anxiously awaited his next offering. At 246 pages, *Mongol!* ran very long for a pornographic paperback, which averaged 170 pages at the time. The retrospective narrator is Chepi Noyan, son of a lowly blacksmith who rises to the rank of general under Genghis Khan. The book begins with direct address, which creates a closeness, a sense of trust, as Chepi draws the reader into his perceptions.

> *The story I have to tell you is not of love, nor of peace and tranquility. Such was not my destiny, and there was none such while my lord Jenghis lived.*

At its best, *Mongol!* is a young man's adventure tale. Chepi is a laconic warrior, a man of swift action, and the book has little dialogue. Prolonged scenes of battle depict the brilliant tactics of lofting arrows between lines of cavalry. Communication is carried out by colored flags and blasts from a horn. After battle comes the glory, always sexual.

The longest chapter portrays an arranged marriage that begins with a fake sword fight between Chepi and the bride's father, followed by her "escape." Encountering her fierce resistance, Chepi realizes that she wants the full ritual carried out in the ancient fashion. She wants to be raped. This is emblematic of much of my father's work—a woman who desires forceful sex—but in *Mongol!*,

Dad relies on cultural precedent to write a two-page rape scene, including tips on how to deflower a virgin.

The language of sex in American English is relegated to medical terminology or the gutter. It's a kind of dialect that everyone knows. Today it is stereotypical, but in 1970 my father was at the vanguard of creating an idiom destined to become comical cliché. Each noun and verb received the gift of a modifier. A penis was always an anxious shaft, a turgid member, a throbbing rod, or an aching lance. A vagina was a welcoming sheath, a swollen cleft, a humid channel. The verbs shifted by gender. Men's actions were variations of thrust, lunge, plunge, or impale, whereas women tended to writhe, moan, quiver, shiver, and quake.

Dad often told me that he was the top in his field, the most prolific, the classiest operator, the highest-paid. I've since learned that other people wrote more, and some were better. His actual legacy may be the rare exclamatory title, a device he used far more than any other pornographer. *Mongol!* was his first, followed by:

Asking for It!
Begging for It!
Brother, Darling!
Disciplined!
Jonuta Rising!
MANLIB!
Peggy Wants It!
Pleasure Us!
Snatch Me!
The 8-Way Orgy!

Initially I considered it a standard trope of marketing; however, most of these books came from different publishers. A random sampling was necessary, and Dad's personal collection of six hundred porn novels served my purpose. Not a single one offered an exclamation point.

I reread *Mongol!*, skipping the sex scenes to focus on the story. What emerged was a detailed and dramatic narrative of military conquest, related by a lonely man. Chepi often sits in his tent, drinking liquor and ruminating about the past. He is perpetually at war with the world, living in self-imposed solitude. His only sources of comfort are alcohol, cruelty, and sex—as if predicting my father's future life.

Chepi cannot make a woman pregnant, a source of personal anguish. He repeatedly laments his "empty quiver." Without sex, the book becomes a tragic portrait of a warrior bereaved by the absence of what he most wants—a son to ride after him, to carry on—in a very real sense, to do what I did with my own work.

My second reading of *Mongol!* furthered the deterioration of the brittle yellow pages. The cover tore away from the dried glue of the spine, and I discovered the following inscription on the title page:

For Helen Offutt, perennial fan.
[signed] John 9/1970

Astonished, I mentally traced the book's provenance—this was the very copy Dad had given his mother. He'd recovered it after her death and kept it until he died, whereupon it came to me. Like the DNA of Genghis Khan, Dad's novel had passed through generations. I tried to imagine my grandmother sitting on her veranda with a glass of sweet tea, reading *Mongol!* Perhaps she heeded his warning and remained cloistered behind the barricade of index cards blocking the sex scenes. But I doubt it. How could she, or anyone, not be tempted to peek?

Later that day I visited Mom and asked why Dad had sent

Mongol! to his mother. Mom speculated that he'd spoken with her about his research: "Like you talk to me," she said, "for the book about your father."

I told her I was worried she might not like what I was writing, that she loved Dad in a certain way, was in love with him, but my relationship was different. I was interested in him as a writer and father, not as a husband. She asked if I wanted her to read it. I shook my head and she seemed disappointed. I realized she was simply offering to do what she'd always done for Dad—read the material before publication. Mom wanted to be useful.

"You know," I said, "Dad was the most interesting character I've ever met."

"Yes, he was. A mass of contradictions."

"Do you think he was lonely?"

"Funny you mention that," she said. "I asked him the same thing once. He got very intense. You know how he did that with his eyes and his voice. And he said, 'Not anymore.' It was about the nicest compliment he ever gave me."

We looked at each other silently; our conversations often contain quiet periods of private thought followed by jokes and laughter. My mother and I share a sense of humor. She is a good companion in any situation, flexible and adaptive, always cheerful.

A car trundled by outside. A dog barked. I was tired. I stood to go and my mother stood, as well. She approached the bookshelf where she kept a few of Dad's novels, my books, my wife's poetry, and the textbooks my aunt and brother wrote. Mom pulled my first published book off the shelf, then put it back.

"No," she said, "that one was for your father and me."

She found another copy of *Kentucky Straight*.

"This one's mine," she said. "You gave it to me when I taught at the prison. Do you remember doing that?"

"No, I don't."

"And you worry about my memory," she said. "Maybe yours isn't as good as you think."

"Maybe not."

She opened the book to the flyleaf and read it silently. "Every time I look at it," she said, "it makes me smile."

She showed me the inscription.

To Mom,
There's nobody I'd rather see than you.
[signed] Chris Offutt, 11/93

I told her it was still true. I hugged her and said goodbye. She waved from the doorway as I backed out into the street. I drove home thinking about two different books, two different mothers, and two different sons. Giving Mom her own copy of *Kentucky Straight* was an effort to seek approval. I also wanted her to read about the world in which she'd raised me, an environment she didn't understand, harsher than she knew. Maybe my father had a similar impulse. He wanted his mother to know she'd raised a son who wrote dirty books.

Chapter Twenty-one

DESPITE LIFELONG difficulties with my father, I lived for his attention. The only behavior that earned it was writing, which I began at age seven, eventually completing forty short stories before leaving home a decade later. I gave all the manuscripts to Dad, and he returned them with corrections. The lessons were mainly grammatical, but notes on structure and characterization were often embedded within his comments. Very occasionally I found lines of praise, which thrilled me for days. I transformed these slim kudos into proof that my father loved me as much as I loved him.

In 1985 Dad was under severe pressure from his publisher to produce books in his *Spaceways* series, a blend of pornography and science fiction. Despite his ability to write fast, he was falling behind on a deadline of a book per month. His solution was to find collaborators who'd write a novel to be published under Dad's pseudonym of John Cleve. He would pay a few thousand dollars, edit their manuscripts, and take full copyright. He sent me a letter asking if I'd write one. His offer pleased me with its implied recognition of my skills as a writer, and I spent a lot of time composing my response. I couldn't tell him the truth—I absolutely did not want to begin my career ghostwriting my father's porn.

From Dad's perspective, he was offering to help his son, the struggling writer who could use the money. He and Mom had expressed concern about my choice of employment. I was a twenty-five-year-old dishwasher in Salem, Massachusetts, working fifteen hours a week for minimum wage, supplemented by all the food I could eat. I had no phone or car, rode my bicycle in all weather, and lived in an extremely cheap apartment. On the wall of my room I fastened a mirror directly above my typewriter. Surrounding the mirror were photographs of writers whose work I admired. My only hope of joining their company was sitting at the typewriter. If I didn't write, the mirror was empty. It was a powerful inducement to work.

My roommates were a visual artist and a physicist. We were good friends and got along well. The physicist spent fifteen hours a week commuting to and from work—the same amount of time I worked—but at the end of the month he always ran out of money. I took great pleasure in lending him cash. We were young men in our twenties, prone to elaborate pranks and an occasional drunken food fight. At times we got on one another's nerves.

I wrote to Dad, referring in a casual way to this dynamic. The bulk of the letter was a polite refusal of his offer to write under his pseudonym. As diplomatically as I could, I explained that I was working on a book of my own and wanted to concentrate on finishing it. Dad quickly responded with a letter that didn't mention the *Spaceways* series but focused on my shortcomings as a person who shared living quarters.

It seems to me that it's up to me, after all these years, to tell you this. Two words will do it, Chris: You lurch.

Maybe "You lunge" is closer. It is both a physical and emotional trait, often known as response to a tap on the knee, shortened to kneejerk. I would not care to try to read in a room with you; hell, even to live in a house with you without a soundproof retreat.

I touch my cat nicely & see her kneejerk mind: "Touch/ love/stroke/warm/belly/food" & she lunges to rush to her bowl. Single-minded & inconsiderate ("I'm being nice to you, asshole; what makes you think I wish to inspect your rapidly receding anus?!")

You are upstairs, & wish to be down. You start but tarry because something catches your attention. You inspect/ peruse it. <u>Och! I wished to be downstairs</u>, you suddenly think. You lurch, lunge, race. Your shoes are angry hammers, attacking each step as an enemy. All others within the house are disrupted: that neither occurs to nor concerns you. Got-To-Get-Downstairs.

<u>Food</u>. The thought hits. You lurch, lunge to the refrigerator with considerable noise. You lurch-jerk open the door. In lunges a hand to thrust things around. A vocal sound. Another. Ah. You jerk it out. Bang it down. That which you have jerked out & banged down has a lid. With a vocal sound you wrench it off, drop it. Lurch, feet slapping, legs churning in an un-ignorable <u>palpable</u> breeze & corner-of-the-eye-visible blur of lurching movement, to the [stove/sink/counter/table].

You "decide" abruptly (the knee does) to sing or whistle. At volume. Single-minded & inconsiderate.

Scenario:
   two or 3 people are in a room talking (variant 1)

   one person is in a room (variant 2) reading/listening to a piece of music/news/voice/sound

   (sub-variant 2)
                          or
   thinking out a story/idea/thought/painting/good or bad/idea

   (sub-variant 3)
                          and
   You enter the room, very rapidly, talking. Single-minded, inconsiderate, & lurchy. From thought to thought; from dream to dream; from plan to "plan"; from stillness to movement to stillness. (Stillness—usually with from one to three bodily parts in movement, catching the peripheral vision, maddeningly, of anyone around.)

Like, man, you <u>distract</u> alla time, man. It's impossible to be around (near; in the same stadium with) you & not be <u>aware</u> of you. No talk of moodiness; no use of the o'erused adjective mercurial; it's the inability to be alone and have private space, even for the eyes.

I'll hand this to your mama tomorrow; if she considers it too strong, I'll send it anyhow.

I have never been able to resist: I have never met anyone
I cared about whom I didn't try to change.

[signed]
—Himself

The letter devastated me for days. Wondering if anything in it was true, I showed the pages to my roommates. They had problems with their own fathers, but nothing of this magnitude, and were shocked by the contents. One roommate suggested I burn the letter on the beach. The other roommate assured me none of it was valid. His only complaint about me was that I stayed in my room too much, writing. They treated me with a rough sympathy, but sadness had settled into me. I felt helpless, despising myself for being so vulnerable to Dad eight years after leaving home.

By then I had the habit of preserving anything I received from my father, and I slipped the letter into a file folder and tucked it away. Rereading the pages now, I can see that it was motivated by my refusal to write a *Spaceways* book for him. Turning down his offer implied personal rejection. Faced with such imagined evaluation, he attacked.

Over the years I continued to try to connect with my father, but the letter lay between us, never remarked upon. Mom acted as go-between, telling me that the tension bothered Dad. I knew that no conversation with her was private, that he expected a detailed report of any communication. My response was painful to both Mom and me—I stopped talking to her about anything meaningful. I never showed her the letter or confronted Dad about it. Doing so would further difficulties that became known in the family as "the trouble."

When my siblings called home, Dad complained about me, placing them in an uncomfortable position. They were performing their duty as he demanded, only to hear his grievances toward me instead of interest in their lives. He cast himself as the long-suffering victim of what he called my "professional rebellion." Dad blamed me for our distance and tried for years to recruit my siblings to his side.

After he died, we all became closer. For the first time in forty-three years, the family enthusiastically gathered in Mississippi for a Thanksgiving meal.

Chapter Twenty-two

IN OXFORD, Mom fainted a couple of times and began wearing a heart monitor. I called more often, feeling a twinge of anxiety if she didn't answer. One day I called twice in an hour and it went to voicemail. I was driving to her house when she called me back and apologized.

"I was on the phone," she said. "I'm ordering something from Victoria's Secret."

"Okay, Mom."

"What do you think of that?"

"Uh, no comment."

She laughed. "I have to go now," she said. "I'm watching the Reds. It's tied in the ninth."

"Would you like me to come watch with you?"

"Yes," she said. "No. It's over. That rat bastard got a hit. Goodbye."

I returned home and began sifting through my father's work once more. At the time of his careful filing, he wouldn't have known that a son would search it for clues and information. The essential DNA of my father lay arrayed on pages before me. This undertaking hasn't brought me closer to him. If anything, it's a constant reminder that no matter who I think I am, I will always be my father's son. I don't know if I'm a writer because of him or in spite of him. If my life has been motivated by rebellion against my father, what have I gained through the liberty of his demise? A newfound sense of life? No. The intrinsic joy in little things? No.

I don't miss my father, but without his shackles to strain against, the world is terrifying and vast. I have lost a kind of purpose, a reason to prove myself.

In an article written for *Trumpet,* a science fiction fanzine from the early sixties, my father declared his credentials as a suitable columnist—he'd read every word of Havelock Ellis, Sigmund Freud, and the Marquis de Sade. A subsequent letter to the editor criticized Dad for bragging, and implied that he had lied. I located the books in question. They spanned fourteen inches of shelf space, tall books with hundreds of thin pages. Dad had annotated them heavily, writing comments in response like a form of Midrash. He argued with Freud but not Ellis. The books by de Sade held fewer comments but had more sections marked by brackets and exclamation points. Passages that validated sexual domination were consistently marked. Though he may have begun in an earnest quest for knowledge, his marginalia indicated that he wound up finding confirmation of his own ideas, like a zealot with a sacred text. My father sought formal evidence that his sexual fascism was normal and everyone else had it wrong.

Dad's sense of cruelty and judgment came from an antiquated mode of Catholicism. He constructed a cross of porn and kept himself tightly affixed to it, suffering for his own obsessions. He exchanged heaven and hell for reincarnation, but the abyss of his shame was pure Roman Catholic. Sex was filthy. Expiation was necessary. The outlet of writing porn was a relief from the guilt brought on by writing porn, a kind of Mobius strip—never-ending and self-perpetuating.

Growing up in a house with sexuality simmering beneath the surface—books, pamphlets, art on the walls, and Dad's regular comments—instilled in me a yearning to be a ladies' man. In high school I never had a girlfriend, and I'd had only one during college. My experience with the fatman left me passive, unwilling to try to seduce women. I didn't want to place a female in a similar situation—uncertain and scared, unable to halt the proceedings, utterly disengaged emotionally. If I liked a woman, which was rare, since most people bored me, I spent enough time with her until she finally made the first move.

Many years later in Salem, Massachusetts, my roommate tried to teach me how to pick up women in bars, an effort I never adequately mastered. It appeared to be a complex and false rigmarole, as if those involved were seeking sexual partners while trying to pretend they weren't. My roommate offered many tips but was aghast at my inability to read basic signals. I never knew if a woman found me attractive, and simply assumed she didn't.

In the manner of Cyrano, my roommate attempted assistance. At a local corner tavern called In a Pig's Eye, a woman asked me what I did. It was a straightforward question, common in banal conversation, but I had no idea how to answer. The truth was I did nothing but read books, ride my bicycle, and try to write. At the time I wasn't even sure what she meant—what does anyone do? We mark time until we die.

She was still waiting for an answer. My roommate filled the silence.

"He's a writer," he said.

"Oh," she said. "What does he write about?"

"His dick."

She gave me a sharp look and said, "That sounds like pornography."

"No," my roommate said. "If he writes about other people's dicks, it's porn. But if it's his own, it's art."

The two of them began a lively conversation, later leaving together, and that was as close as I ever got to picking up a woman in a bar.

To get the details straight about the Salem anecdote, I needed access to my journals, which went back forty-five years. They were stacked floor-to-ceiling in a closet, cartons that contained everything I'd written since second grade. Boxes of my father's work blocked the closet door. My own archives were carefully taped and labeled, but the journal I sought was out of place. I found it inside an unlabeled carton that held a short story I'd forgotten about. My literary archive wasn't as organized as I thought—much like Dad's.

To find the Salem section, I read dozens of entries written at a frantic pace, accounts of beleaguered woe and complaint. No matter how far back I looked into my own life, the rapid scrawl covered the same subjects: I felt bad, I didn't like what I wrote, I hated myself. I resolved to burn the journals. Then I decided not to.

I'd grown up in the country, run from it for most of my life, and now wanted to live nowhere else. Between ages nineteen and fifty-three, I traveled relentlessly, living and working in New York City, Boston, Paris, Florida, Iowa, Georgia, Tennessee, Arizona, New Mexico, Montana, Kentucky, California, and Mississippi. In my free time I visited other places. I'd slept in every state except North Dakota and Delaware and still hoped to get there.

What began as a desire to see the other side of the nearest hill at home had shifted to travel as a habitual way of life. If things didn't work out, I moved on. I knew how to arrive in a new town, get a job, find a cheap room, and furnish it with junk from the street. I liked living without history, nothing held against me. My brother once asked what I was running from. I told him I wasn't, I was running toward, only I didn't know toward what. He nodded and said, "You'll always be afraid of him, you know."

I didn't believe my brother, didn't want to, couldn't bear to face the idea. It took courage to live my way—hitchhiking across the country, refusing to take a full-time job. I wasn't afraid of anything except snakes, and I'd killed one and skinned it and hung the brittle hide on a nail where I could see it every day in order to overcome my phobia. But my brother was right all along. I didn't know it until my fear ended with Dad's death.

I became concerned that examining the minutiae of his work was turning me into him. I wrote ten hours a day. At night I read. I avoided leaving the house. I got mad at small things, yelled at inanimate objects. If this were true—the steady evolution to becoming Dad—then my sons will suffer the same fate and become me, an absurd notion that destroys the logic of my premise. Therefore, I am not my father. I'm a middle-aged man contemplating my own mortality through the lens of a parent's death.

I went outside and watched two sparrows fight in my dusty gravel driveway. On a distant fence post, a hawk watched them. The air thickened suddenly and a quick shower pocked the dirt. The birds flew away and the hawk moved on. The rain stopped. I headed for the woods behind my house. I walked a quarter mile to a barbed wire fence that had been mended several times.

Going through a barbed wire fence is a simple skill. Like swimming or riding a bicycle, once learned it's never forgotten. I crouched, pressed the low wire down with one hand, stepped over it, and carefully eased my body through the gap. Twice I felt the barbs scrape my shirt, but I was moving slowly enough to stop, bend my knee a quarter inch lower, and pass through safely.

I walked the length of a fallow cotton field to the edge of Berry Branch, a very old creek with a ten-foot bank running nearly straight down. Water moved slowly along the sandy bottom. Kudzu had killed several smaller trees. A large maple lay in the creek, its roots eroded from below. I headed west to a series of smaller gullies where I'd found feather and bone before.

A shape that didn't fit in caught my peripheral attention. I stopped moving, fearful of a snake, and saw a turtle as wide as my hand. It had been climbing a bank before I arrived. Now it had halted, blending in like a stone, its head protruding from the gray shell, back legs extended on the slight incline. As a boy I'd caught dozens of turtles, carried them home, and kept them in a cardboard box with grass and water until realizing they were the most boring pet of all. I painted the back of their shells with fingernail polish, then set them free, hoping to find one again.

I wondered if this particular turtle had seen a human before. I squatted a few feet away and asked where he'd been and where he was going. I warned him about water moccasins and coyotes. I told him about my father. After twenty minutes my knee was cramped and the turtle hadn't answered. He stayed immobile during our entire conversation. I told him goodbye and headed home, momentarily cheered.

I walked across the field and passed through the fence without a scratch. Crawling along my arm was a Lone Star tick, with the distinctive yellow spot on its back. I cut it in half with my thumbnail. At home I removed my muddy boots and drank some water. Briefly I wondered what my neighbors would think if they'd come upon me while conversing with a turtle. They'd probably have watched silently, then slipped away. Everyone on the road would know, but nobody would mind. In Mississippi personal eccentricity didn't matter any more than it did in Kentucky. I'd found a home, the same as Dad had in the hills.

Chapter Twenty-three

FOR THIRTY years my father anticipated his impending death—*at any time!*—and suggested that family members earmark objects in the house by taping our names on them. None of us did. For me it felt morbid, as if competing with my siblings for threadbare rugs might hasten his demise.

In 1998 I relocated to Kentucky one last time, filled with optimism and hope. I bought a house high on a hill with a long balcony overlooking several acres and a pond, the nicest home I'd ever had. Prior to this, my wife and young sons had lived in a string of cheap dumps rented over the phone, moving our increasingly battered secondhand belongings. Although I didn't know it yet, my marriage was deeply troubled by the itinerant lifestyle of a perpetually visiting writer at various universities. We made seven interstate moves in four years, saving the boxes each time. As the adventure wore off, so did the sheen of marital bliss.

This was intended as the final move—back to Kentucky at age forty for a permanent job at my alma mater, Morehead State University. We needed furniture, and I decided to take my father up on his largess. He always said I could have anything, but I had never asked. This would be a first.

Visiting my folks' house was always fraught with tension from the onset. When was the best time? How much notice did Dad need? Not too early, not too late, no time was ever ideal. If I took my sons along, I left them in the car while I entered the house and put the guns away. Dad didn't like that. He suggested I should've taught my sons not to touch guns.

"They're little kids," I said. "They might accidentally run into the shotgun by the door."

"They won't run in my house!"

"I don't meant run literally, but you know how boys play."

"Then they can play outside."

"Mom might want them to come in and eat."

Dad walked away without speaking. I knew that evoking my mother had won the initial skirmish, but he would resent it for the entire visit.

Next came the production of pouring bourbon. It was best if Dad picked the glass, because any I chose was deemed inappropriate: too old, too new, reserved for special occasions, or a longtime favorite now retired. Preparing drinks gave my father the opportunity to talk nonstop while establishing dominion over the kitchen, the house, and the glassware—but mainly over me.

Equipped with whiskey, we went to the living room, where I listened to his criticism of politics, my siblings, and TV programming. I gulped my drink, which Dad would comment on—*chip off the old block, son*—and at the slightest lull in his monologue, I hurried to the kitchen, tossed back a shot of liquor, filled my glass, and returned to the living room. Dad resumed talking at the precise point he'd stopped, often in midsentence, a trait I found impressive.

Years back, Mom had replaced the dining room set and gotten

rid of the old ladder-backed chairs with seats woven of rush. I'd grown up with five chairs at the table instead of six because Dad used one in his office. My parents had enclosed the side porch for storage, and suspended by a hook on the wall was the last dining room chair, dusty and laced with cobwebs. Dad raised the inevitable subject of what I'd like from the house. I suggested the chair, believing there'd be no conflict, since it was clearly not in use.

"What chair?" he said.

"On the wall out there."

"No. That one has to stay."

"Does Mom want it?"

"No, I do! That was John Cleve's chair. He retired and his chair did, too. Ol' John's gone. That chair deserves a rest."

After Dad died, I cleared the storage room but left the chair on the wall. Mom mentioned it and I reminded her it had been John Cleve's and she dropped the subject. My sisters talked of burning it. I considered a formal pyre, but the outdoor fireplace had long since collapsed, and the living room contained a woodstove that hadn't been used in so long, it contained the mummified corpses of eleven birds. My brother was surprised I wanted to keep the chair, but I couldn't bring myself to throw it out. It was less a case of loyalty to my father than to the chair itself and, in a circuitous way, to literature. The chair deserved more than flame. It had served. Two months later I moved it to Mississippi.

I made space in my writing room for Dad's executive desk, opposite my own desk, made of plywood over sawhorses. Mine contrasted starkly with his. A set of deep drawers flanked the knee hole, and a wide pencil drawer spanned the top. I oiled the metal slides, waxed the wooden runners, and polished the surface to a shiny gleam. I tucked John Cleve's chair into the knee hole. The front legs were scraped and dented, but the chair was intact, the nails firm, the glue tight. His desk became a catch-all for papers, slowly collecting dust as if unable to get free of old behavior. I never sat in the chair. No one had but Dad until he hung it on the wall.

When it came time to organize a file of Dad's earliest artwork, I was reluctant to again take over the dining room table. The light was poor, and working there disrupted meals. My own desk was small, with notes and paper cluttering the surface. The best option was my father's desk. I stared at Ol' John's chair for a long time, imagining my father hunched over the surface of the desk, working furiously.

I went outside to smoke a cigarette. I emptied the trash. I washed my face and combed my hair. I picked up my father's chair and readjusted it. I walked back and forth behind it like a dog. I ate a piece of chocolate. I considered another cigarette. Then I smoked one. I thought of all the things I'd done that were supposedly brave:

Faced a man with a loaded gun.
Entered numerous cars with strangers while hitchhiking.
Camped alone in the woods.
Killed a poisonous snake with a stick.
Moved to cities where I didn't know anyone.
Slept in a cemetery at night.
Hopped a train.
Defended myself with my fists.
Explored a house supposedly haunted.
Talked my way out of being mugged.
Ran a chainsaw.
Lived in a foreign country.
Crawled out of waist-deep quicksand.
Rappelled headfirst down a cliff.

I finished the cigarette, came inside, and wrote the preceding list. These were not acts of genuine courage, but were born of foolishness and despair. I was lucky to escape being maimed or killed.

Nothing in my life came close to the courage my father displayed at the age of thirty-six when he quit a successful business career to write books. I was a grown man afraid of furniture. The shame of cowardice compelled me to approach the desk. I withdrew the chair, and I sat. Nothing untoward happened. It was just an old chair, not real comfortable.

I began reading *Marcus Severus in Ancient Rome,* a black-and-white comic book Dad made at age seventeen. To avoid capture, Marcus becomes the first man to swim the English Channel. He evades opposing forces and heads for Rome, accompanied by an "amorous concubine" disguised as a man. The book stops, incomplete, corresponding with his second year of college. That same year his father died of a stroke.

In 1949 Dad began another comic, *Cade of the Galactic Patrol,* and worked on it for nine years. The narrative is swiftly engaging. Richard Louis Cade, an officer in the Grand Army of the Galactic Republic, goes on a mission to rescue the president's daughter. In a portent of contemporary times, people talk on "vizi-phones" and transmit instant "galactic telegrams" via desktop computers.

A strange dreamlike quality pervades the crude art. Perspective and scale are off-kilter. Figures exist independently of the space they inhabit. Backgrounds are vaguely rendered in repeating patterns of crosshatching and tightly compressed vertical lines. Characters change clothes often. A fierce warrior woman goes about dressed as a boy, while Cade wears loose blouses and midthigh skirts because his "clothes are at the cleaners."

Dad finished the final installment of *Cade* a few months after I was born. On the last page, Cade looks in a mirror, experiencing his only self-reflective moment in 230 pages.

He sees himself ten years ago entering the Space Academy and beginning his career, expecting to be either dead or

married and settled . . . and where am I? Neither dead or
settled. Or maybe I am dead—

It is tempting to freight these words with retrospective
meaning—is my father suggesting that marriage or paternity made
him feel dead? The word "cade" means an animal abandoned by its
mother and raised by humans, a kind of feral foundling. Perhaps
Cade's literal comment "maybe I am dead" is how Dad always
felt. Then again, maybe it's just a comic book made by a twenty-
four-year-old late at night after a long day's work, drinking Schlitz
and smoking cigarettes while his new wife soothes his infant son.
Regardless of interpretation, Dad never returned to Cade. In his
notes, he wrote that he quit because it was veering toward the
shameful.

Dad often told me that a writer's earliest work was his best
because he put his entire life into it. All subsequent writing contained the accumulation of a few years at best. With that in mind
I sat down to read "Population Implosion," the 1967 short story
that brought him attention in the science fiction field. Reflected
on the pages was my father's personality as I remembered it from
my childhood—energetic, funny, concerned, serious, and original.
At the end I began to cry. Each time my sobs faded, the emotion
forced its way out again. I finally subsided, gasping for breath,
drained and clearheaded. I'd kept my grief tightly stowed for
months and now felt relieved. I understood that I was mourning
my father but not his death. I wept for the talent he had as a young
man, the great writer he might have become.

My father's best work was from 1966 to 1972, before the pace
at which he wrote began to affect quality. On some level he knew
this was true. Aside from *Mongol!*, two other early novels received
his positive evaluation, both written in the late sixties. In his notes
he wrote: "*Captives in the Chateau de Sade* is the one I assume will

be a classic, to be reprinted in the next century and the next, over or under the counter depending upon the politics and mood of the time." The book has many literary allusions, extremely rare in porn, including Stendhal, Freud, and de Sade. The protagonist instructs his followers in the treatment of their sexual prisoners:

> *Remember this: it is caprice and lack of emotion that defeats them. When you show them emotion, of any kind, they feel a burst of accomplishment and pride.*

Dad gave me his other favorite during my early twenties, saying *Bruise* was his concept of an intellectual look at S&M. The novel is set in my family home in the woods and features a protagonist who thinks and talks like my father. *Bruise* is a realistic depiction of two couples who kidnap five young people and sexually torture them to death. The pace is slow and deliberate, allowing a psychological depth missing from his other novels. The ending is an equally significant departure, never again seen in his work: regret for having murdered innocent people.

Dad's unpublished novels surpass twenty-five, more than most authors can claim for their life's output. In the late 1960s, my father wrote his finest book, the never-published *Autobiography of a Sex Criminal*. It is Dad's only novel that includes the point of view of a child—the narrator's early years as he evolves into a sexual serial killer. The protagonist is smart, educated, and able to function in society. He plans ahead and preys on vulnerable hitchhikers. Sexual satisfaction is linked to homicide and postmortem mutilation. He often rearranges the victims' clothes afterward. These are standard tropes of television and movies today, but at the time Dad wrote, the FBI hadn't started its Behavioral Science Unit. The term "serial killer" hadn't been invented yet. My father imagined his way into all of it—childhood deprivation and obsession, followed by initial bloodletting, a crime of opportunity, then more careful planning, stalking, and ritualized homicide.

Dad's papers held a brief note saying: "Unbought because it is ugly, and tries to Say Something." The "something" was his belief that the penal system was too lenient and criminals were getting smarter. I think editors rejected it because it didn't accomplish the essential task of fetish porn—sufficiently titillating the reader's desire to masturbate. It is too well written and the sex scenes are too brutal.

Another unpublished manuscript is my father's earliest story and the sole work intended to be literary. It has two separate title pages. One says "The Other Side of the Story" by Andy Offutt. The second one, used on the final manuscript, is "Requite Me, Baby" by Morris Kenniston. Dad was twenty when he wrote it, just prior to graduating from the University of Louisville.

In the past fifteen years, I've taught creative writing at a number of universities, colleges, and conferences. If I'd come across this story in my teaching, I would have considered it among the most promising works I'd seen. A remarkable intelligence operates behind the prose. The subject of Dad's story is a couple's breakup, but the man can't bring himself to end the relationship. He doesn't want to hurt his girlfriend. Instead, he mentally harangues himself as a coward for being trapped by social expectation. Dad experiments with style by dropping every single comma and using capitalization to indicate the protagonist's thoughts. The voice is reminiscent of contemporary writers at the time, a combination of Salinger and Hemingway.

One strong note is his handling of time. The entire story occurs in approximately fifteen seconds, during which two characters utter seven short lines of dialogue. The rest of the story consists of the man's thoughts. In that brevity, an entire world is created, a conflict arises within the well-defined protagonist, and the midcentury era is fully evoked.

If I were a teacher conferring with the twenty-year-old who wrote it, I'd be extremely supportive. I'd affirm that he was a good writer, that he'd obviously spent an inordinate amount of time reading and writing. Keep on experimenting, I'd say, but focus on structure and character instead of punctuation. You're a good writer, I'd tell him, you could be a great writer. Don't squander your talent. Don't let it trickle away.

Chapter Twenty-four

MY FATHER had a compulsive need to express every opinion he ever had. All were judgments and most were negative. I once saw him hurt his fingers while opening a can of fruit in the kitchen. Enraged, he flung the metal can opener, claiming that the manufacturer had deliberately made it in such a way to attack him personally. *The designer should be shot!* I nodded dutifully.

An inveterate writer of letters, he sent out weekly missives of complaint. For serious issues, he used carbon paper and saved the letter on translucent sheets of onionskin. Among the earliest was to *Newsweek* magazine, dated July 8, 1964, a week after my youngest sister was born. The letter was his reply to a recent article by Monsignor Kelly of New York, who'd denounced the widespread use of birth control pills.

Dad begins his letter by referring to himself as a fertile Catholic with three unplanned children, proving the ineffectiveness of the rhythm method. He quotes the monsignor's statement that "The sex organs were made by God to reproduce the human race." Dad responds:

It follows that not using the sex organs to reproduce the race is a man-made sin. It therefore follows that Msgr Kelly is guilty of a great and deliberate sin; he is not using his.

He goes on to excoriate the editors of *Newsweek* for running a one-sided article. Unsurprisingly, those same editors refrained from printing the letter, which irked Dad for years.

Subsequent letters went to bankers, lawyers, corporate executives, religious leaders, two presidents, three governors, several senators, newspapers, magazines, radio stations, hospitals, TV networks, the U.S. postmaster general, the local high school principal, and university administrators. Most of those letters were lost. Dad saved the responses, and therein lie the reactions of citizens caught in his crosshairs. The head of a medical center apologized profusely for making him wait an hour to see a doctor. A potato chip company sent him a case of products after Dad complained about the ratio of air to chips in the bag. President Reagan thanked him for supporting the invasion of Grenada. A radio announcer for local Little League baseball changed his repertoire of descriptive terms based on a list supplied by Dad. Staffs of governors and senators replied. A letter to President Lyndon Johnson complaining about the IRS received a series of responses from the attorney general of the United States, the state director of the IRS, and the regional office in Ashland.

The sheer number of responses reminded me of a dog that barks at passing cars. The cars continue by, confirming to the dog that he has successfully chased the vehicle away, a reward that leads to barking at the next car. Trainers teach dogs to halt this habit through the technique of leash popping, but my father remained unleashed throughout his life. His only tether was the limit of his outrage.

As I read his correspondence, I saw a pattern begin to emerge. He opened with bullying, then followed by announcing his qualifications, at times invented, always enhanced. Here is the opening paragraph to an editor, dated 1982, on the subject of a proposed title change for a novel.

> *Without having met, we seem to have gained the*
> *wrong idea about each other. I am neither a beginner,*
> *a coolie, nor a piece of dough for your rolling pin. I*
> *am a relatively human being with a few university*
> *degrees, over thirty novels, and even some class. Not*
> *since 1971 has any treated me so callously as you have*
> *done.*

I also found more than fifty letters to copy editors. Dad believed that criticizing in advance would allow him to get his way. The following is a excerpt.

> *Over the course of a lot of years I have come to*
> *think of myself as a professional. My degrees are*
> *in English, psychology, and linguistics. I have*
> *not misspelled a word—unless intentionally—*
> *in thirty years. Nor do I make mistakes in*
> *punctuation.*

I suspect that his ongoing combat with copy editors was a self-perpetuating cycle. Dad insulted them and they disobeyed his orders, which refreshed his anger.

Occasionally I found a copy of a letter Dad sent seeking work, in one case to an editor of fetish booklets that featured photographs and text:

> *Enclosed is the third draft of a very unusual manuscript. I am a writer, and know my way around the areas of erotica, sadism, and masochism—if they can ever be separated.*
>
> *My chief gripe when I've received books from you is that I've wondered why in heck the stories and pictures couldn't match. So—I did it. Not only is it a story that looks as if the pictures were specifically taken to go with it, but it's better written than yours.*
>
> *I can do this with any adequate set of pictures, in any 7-day period or less. How far in advance do you work? The idea fascinates me.*
>
> *Terms?*

There are no follow-up letters or copies of the booklets he wrote. Possibly his approach foundered with the suggestion that he was a better writer than those currently employed by the publisher.

Of the nearly twenty thousand letters I examined, many were Dad's responses to fan mail. Every letter opened with the salutation "offutt to _____, peace," an affectation borrowed from the counter-culture. Dad wasn't a hippie and certainly never sought peace. He was at war with himself. The battlefield was anyone handy, and fans were vulnerable. Below is an opening line typical of his responses to fan mail.

> *Never mind what others would not do; my own rules forbid me to respond to someone arrogant enough not to send me return postage for a reply. Obviously I have more empathy than sense, and make you this gift.*

A very long fan letter came from a seventy-five-year-old man who'd assisted in his wife's suicide rather than prolong her suffering from terminal cancer. His letter praised Dad's porn and asked how to get more John Cleve books. A postscript pointed out a grammatical error in one of Dad's novels. Dad responded thusly:

> *Yes, of course it is nitpicking to PS an otherwise nice letter, requesting time and money/effort from a writer— or any other human being, surely—with the quoting of a slip on p. 24 in which "less" appears rather than "fewer."*
> *Nitpicking and dumb, because it is designed to lose friends and intimidate people. Everything else is fascinating though, including the ghastliness of your wife's dying.*

A single file contained hundreds of letters seeking forgiveness for minor transgressions such as misspelling his name. Others were from people seeking clarity about the gross insult for which they'd endured his public admonishment. Many asked if he was angry about a recent interaction. Several apologized for the error of calling him Andy instead of Andrew. In one response Dad explained himself.

> *I remain a bit old-fashioned. That's part of the reason I call you by your full name; I don't haul off and first-name anyone, and indeed dislike having it done. On the other hand, I dislike "Mister."*

This letter remains my favorite for its exemplification of my father's conflicted relationship with himself, played out on strangers. Identity is the central issue, and Dad thinks his way into a room with no exit. Calling him the diminutive Andy is far too intimate an act from a stranger, while using the formal Andrew is not sufficiently old-fashioned. He does not care for Mister Offutt. Technically, no name is left, making me wonder if John Cleve was writing as Dad instead of the other way around.

After reading several thousand letters, I visited my mother. I told her what I'd found and said it was almost like Dad was a crank. She looked at me with a bland expression and said, "You didn't know?"

Chapter Twenty-five

THE COMMERCIAL popularity of American porn novels peaked during the 1970s, coinciding with my father's most prolific and energetic period. In 1972 alone he published eighteen novels. Dad wrote pirate porn, ghost porn, science fiction porn, vampire porn, historical porn, time-travel porn, secret agent porn, thriller porn, zombie porn, and Atlantis porn. An unpublished Old West novel opens with sex in a barn, featuring a gunslinger named Quiet Smith, without doubt Dad's greatest character name. By the end of the decade, Dad claimed to have single-handedly raised the quality of U.S. pornography. According to his private papers, he believed future scholars would refer to him as "King of XX Century Written Pornography."

Many of the early publishers used a "house name," a pseudonym shared by several writers. It concealed identity, which writers preferred, while allowing the publisher to give the illusion of a single author. This was an early attempt at branding, with proven success in other genres. Dad didn't mind, but he was determined to separate himself from others.

His first published novel, before any science fiction, was *Bondage Babes,* released by Greenleaf under the name Alan Marshall in 1968. Payment was six hundred dollars. The plot was a clever conceit. Someone murdered a model for a photographic bondage shoot, and her sister was investigating the crime by posing as a model, which allowed for soft-core descriptions of restrained women. As Dad recalled in a letter:

> *The book was Different: it dared mention clitoris and that some women don't just bop off into orgasm because some dude fills and drills them, and it had a bit of a plot.*

The name John Cleve first appeared on *Slave of the Sudan,* published by Brandon House in 1969, an imitation of Victorian pornography so precisely executed that the editor suspected my father of plagiarism. Dad found this extremely flattering. He published four more novels with Brandon House until it folded.

Dad moved to Orpheus Books, which paid thirteen hundred dollars per book. He used three pseudonyms to conceal his prolificity. Two years later, he switched to Midwood for more money. He invented another pen name, John Denis, based on his favorite Reds players, Johnny Bench and Denis Menke. He published fourteen books with Midwood. After a falling-out with an editor over a title change, he returned to Orpheus. The new editor soon became irritated with Dad and stopped buying his work. Desperate for income, my father invented another pseudonym, Opal Andrews, who specialized in "lightweight incest," and sold eight books to Surrey House.

Curious about the changing market, Dad read a dozen recent Orpheus books, concluding that all were watered-down versions of his own work, his style overtly copied by lesser writers. To him the proof was clear—they'd begun writing about the clitoris. Dad believed he was responsible for the widespread knowledge of its existence in porn, but he couldn't place a book with Orpheus. Outraged, he devised a plan to prove the editor wrong.

To get a different font, he bought a new ball for his Selectric typewriter. He changed his usual margins, used cheaper paper, and rapidly wrote two books as Jeff Morehead. He asked a friend in another part of the country to submit the manuscripts to Orpheus. The editor bought both. Dad called the editor, told him he was Jeff Morehead, and suggested they get back in business. The editor concurred, and Dad stayed with Orpheus throughout the 1970s.

Over the course of his career, he used a total of seventeen pseudonyms:

John Cleve
Turk Winter
Jeff Morehead
Jay Andrews
Opal Andrews
Drew Fowler
J. X. Williams
Jack Cory
Jeremy Crebb
John Denis
Alan Marshall
Jeff Woodson
Joe Brown
Jeff Douglas
Roscoe Hamlin
Camille Colben
Anonymous

Two are female names and six are variations of his own. Three share the initials of J.C., the same as Julius Caesar and Jesus Christ. Dad never quite clarified how he invented the name John Cleve. It first appeared as a character's name in a 1967 manuscript for *Clansman of Andor*. Publicly, Dad claimed John Cleve was a variation of John Cleland, author of *Fanny Hill*, the first pornographic novel printed in English.

In 1973 Grove Press published his novel *The Palace of Venus* under the Zebra imprint. Dad sent them a new novel, *Vendetta*, set during the reign of Pope Innocent III, whom my father characterized as "history's most misnamed monster." The editorial staff didn't want to publish it, and *Vendetta* never saw print, because according to Dad, "It is a class historical and Class is gone." Nevertheless, the strength of the manuscript resulted in a phone call from New York. Barney Rosset, Grove's publisher, wanted a pornographic historical series about a single character during the Crusades. Dad was initially resistant, writing in a letter:

> *I do not know if this is or could be my thing or not. I have difficulty with series. Like, I get bored and want to go back to creating. It is most difficult for me to write as if cranking the arm of a copy-machine. I am an artist, whether these series books will be "art" or not.*

He was equally uncertain about traveling to meet Rosset in New York, a city he called Babylon-on-the-Hudson. Grove offered to cover all expenses and Dad made the trip. He returned to Kentucky with a cash advance, a contract for an unwritten book, and more autonomy than he'd ever had from a publisher. My father had bought Grove books for fifteen years and revered the courage of Rosset for fighting the U.S. government on obscenity charges—and winning. The seventies were financially difficult for

Grove, which barely staved off bankruptcy. Dad regarded his new contract as a mission to save Grove Press. The four-book *Crusader* series sold well, and for the first time in his career, Dad earned royalites.

At the time, pornography was still a taboo business. Paperbacks were sold in the back rooms of adult theaters, on hidden racks at newsstands, and at adult bookstores in cities. People in less-populated areas bought them through the mail. Within a few years of *Crusader*'s publication, Grove suffered further economic problems and the series was in danger of going out of print. Grove wanted to raise the price of Dad's paperbacks one dollar and asked him to cut his royalty percentage in half. If my father didn't agree, Grove couldn't afford to order another printing. Dad got mad and refused, allowing his books to go out of print over the sum of $130 per year, the only professional decision he ever admitted regretting.

In the 1980s, John Cleve's career culminated with a nineteen-book series for Playboy Press, the magazine's first foray into book publishing. *Spaceways* allowed him to blend porn with old-time "space opera" reminiscent of the 1930s pulps, his favorite kind of science fiction. Dad's contemporary twist included aliens who possessed the genitalia of both genders. Galactic crafts welcomed the species as crew, since they could service men and women with ease. The *Spaceways* series ended in 1985, coinciding with the widespread use of consumer VCRs. Men no longer needed "left-handed books" for stimulation when they could watch videotapes in their own homes. The golden era of written pornography was over.

That same year Dad sent *D'Artagnan's Son* to Grove Press, but the pace at which he wrote had finally caught up with him. The prose became sloppy, characterization shrank, and story vanished. A letter of rejection from Grove says:

The problem appears to be that its superior sophistication removes it from the usual market, while its outspoken content might be something of a drawback with the literary crowd. Maybe one way of putting it is that it falls between two chairs.

In my twenty years of writing, I have received nearly six hundred rejections—by mail, phone, email, even text messages. Each one stings. The tendency is always to blame the editor, then oneself, and finally to inspect the language of the rejection letter for hidden meaning. The note my father received resists scrutiny. "Falling between two chairs" is not a conventional literary term or a discernible metaphor. A strict interpretation is that one chair is sophisticated and the other is pornographic, but I remain uncertain as to what lies between them. The editor was probably attempting a diplomatic tone, suggesting the book was too literary for porn and contained too much sex for literature.

The novel opens with a French marquis recalling the death of his first wife while secretly observing his current wife being pleasured by the maid with her "practically prehensile tongue." The marquis's wife is described as having:

> . . . *hectares of black hair, a volcanic vulva and great melonous breasts that shivered and slithered about on her chest, her entire belly a mass of maddeningly molten flesh. Sweat sheened it sleekly.*

The maid leaves the room, encountering the marquis, who promptly takes up with her for several pages. In the meantime, the marquis's wife realizes she has enough time for a liaison with the stable master. On her way, she detours past the kitchen, where the steward is standing on a footstool behind the naked German cook whose backside is in view:

> . . . *her fine big broad plush snowy buttocks standing well out above her sturdy snowy legs, with her also large and snowy breasts out of her bodice.*

Literature has a strong precedent for repetition of words, but I'm not convinced that using "snowy" three times in a single sentence gains sufficient reward. As I read the manuscript, I began to wonder what metaphoric chair it could have landed on to ensure publication.

John Cleve retired in 1985. Dad insisted that he himself hadn't quit, but John Cleve had. It was more retreat than retirement, a slipping back into the shadows, fading away like an old soldier. Cleve had done his duty—the house was paid off, the kids were gone, and the bank held a little savings. Dad was fifty-two. As Cleve, he'd published 130 novels in eighteen years.

Dad continued to write and publish short fiction under his own name, totalling thirty-eight stories between 1954 and 2004. A span of this length is unusual—most writers don't stick with the form for fifty years. On the strength of these publications and his former service as president of the Science Fiction Writers of America, he continued to attend cons, limited to small regional events within driving distance. Ostensibly the reason was practical—Dad couldn't fly due to mysterious pains in his leg—but the truth was far more personal.

In 1972 Harlan Ellison had asked my father to contribute a short story to the influential anthology *Again, Dangerous Visions.* Dad supplied "For Value Received," about a girl who grows up in a hospital because her family can't afford to pay the bill for her birth.

Ellison wrote a respectful introduction to the story, complimenting not only the work but my father's mind, and mentioning that he, Ellison, had entered the same 1954 college science fiction contest that Dad had won. The two men had much in common: They were the same age, from backwaters of Ohio and Kentucky, brilliant, opinionated, articulate, and angry.

In Dad's own introduction to the story, he proclaimed:

> *I love to talk first and write second, and I do both because I have to.*

Many working writers are quite talkative—myself included— eager for social engagement after prolonged solitude. Nevertheless, my father is the only writer I've known who placed talking ahead of writing in importance. Every thought he had was worthy of expression and therefore deserving of a rapt and respectful audience. His family dutifully gave him that, as did fans at small cons.

Inclusion in Ellison's anthology increased my father's profile, and he was asked to serve as Toastmaster for the 1974 World Science Fiction Convention, the most prestigious event in the field. His duties included opening remarks, introducing the guest of honor, and presiding over the Hugo Awards ceremony. Twenty years after his first professional sale and five years after his first con, he'd reached a significant crest in his career. The personal stakes were high. He prepared index cards on which he had bullet points to trigger extemporaneous oration and reduce the chance of sounding canned—replete with dramatic pauses, laugh lines, and grand pronouncements.

At the hotel he dressed in a new leisure suit made of denim with a faux-patch design and flared legs. He wore a white shirt with a broad collar splayed over his suit coat. In the bathroom he trimmed his beard carefully. He double-checked his cuffs, the break of his trousers, and his socks. Accompanied by my mother, who wore a gorgeous white gown, he headed for the banquet.

Worldcon was held in Washington, D.C., at the Sheraton Park Hotel. It had the largest ballroom in the world and had hosted one of the inaugural galas for President Kennedy. By 1974 the infrastructure was disintegrating, and it would soon be torn down. The banquet hall was filled to capacity, with standing room only in the balcony. The air-conditioning failed. The audience was miserably hot, and the hotel staff was unable to resupply pitchers of water at a sufficient rate.

After the meal, Dad commenced his opening remarks about Roger Zelazny, the guest of honor. All went well initially. Perhaps the heat got to my father, or his own anxiety, or he succumbed to the self-destructive pressure he often fought. It could simply have been a case of Dad finally having the floor—the big floor—and he gave over to his love of talking. Whatever the reason, his opening comments began to meander, focusing on himself, and going on too long. Some fans left the room. Others perceived his extended oration as discourteous to Zelazny. People became cranky from the heat and made nasty comments. Open dissent had begun in the audience.

When it became clear that Dad was not moving toward his closing comments, Harlan Ellison decided to intervene. He rose from his spot and began a slow walk toward the head table. Dad ignored him and continued to talk about himself. Ellison reached the podium, motioned to my father and whispered in his ear. The audience erupted with laughter. Dad cut his speech short and Zelazny spoke briefly.

Dad came home incensed at Ellison for interrupting him, the most vile of transgressions against a man who placed talking ahead of every other endeavor. He told me that Ellison had ordered him to pick up the pace. He believed that Ellison was impatient to learn the results of the Hugo Award, for which he had been nominated. Around the house, Dad continually berated Ellison. He made fun of his voice, his height, and his massive ego. *Harlan likes to hurt people. He takes everything personally. He sees everything as a direct challenge.* Even as a teenager, I realized that Dad could be talking about himself.

According to him, the two writers were deeply engaged in a blood feud that would last until one of them died. Diplomatic reconciliation was impossible. Dad's sense of himself was enormous but fragile, as if constructed of bamboo and paper, like a box kite. A slender string tethered it to Earth, and the slightest breeze could knock it astray. His experience at the 1974 Worldcon was a strong enough gust that he never attended another. For the next twenty years, Dad attended only regional cons where fans adored him and were willing to listen without interruption. Upon entering a room, Dad often said in a voice loud enough for everyone to hear: "Is Harlan here? No? Good. Then I'm among friends."

In 2002 Michael Chabon solicited a story from me for a special edition of an anthology entitled *McSweeney's Mammoth Treasury of Thrilling Stories.* Chabon wanted to reinvigorate contemporary literature by bringing his beloved genre tales to the attention of readers. I agreed to contribute and wrote "Chuck's Bucket," a time-travel story based on string theory that explained the existence of ghosts while exploring the possibility of parallel realities. One alternate reality recounted Dad's feud with Ellison.

When the magazine came out, I was in Colorado, preparing to present my work at a writers' conference. I carefully planned my remarks and was attending to my appearance in the mirror when the phone rang in my hotel room. The caller was Harlan Ellison. He'd just read my story and wanted me to know that he had nothing against my father. Stunned, I told him that Dad didn't get along with a lot of people, me included, and Ellison didn't need to sugar-coat things. Ellison said he never sugarcoated anything, *you can ask around,* but insisted that no feud ever existed. He told me he had the utmost respect for my father, whom he considered an excellent writer. He asked me to visit when I was in California, and hung up.

The conversation shocked me, and I thought about it for a long time. Ellison had put forth a degree of effort to track me down at a hotel and make the call. He was known to be rude and irascible, a street fighter in his youth, litigious, a provocateur, and short-tempered. I couldn't summon a reason for him to lie about the feud or about his sincere regard for my father. In short, I believed him. That meant the decades-long conflict was one-sided on my father's part.

I wondered how many other altercations were products of Dad's immense imagination bundled with rage. I'd grown up hearing tales of his disputes, the firing of agents, editors, and collaborators. He had discord with everyone—his mother, his sister, and me. Per-haps he needed foes as much as he needed to talk.

As Dad aged, he outlived the older writers he admired. He had alienated most of his contemporaries, and neglected to befriend the newcomers. All his books were out of print. Invitations to cons dwindled, but Dad told me that he quit fandom due to vanity. He didn't want to be remembered as old and infirm. He was afraid that younger fans wouldn't know who he was, a prospect he couldn't bear.

My brother blamed cons for the erosion of our home life. His reasoning made sense, but I recognized that our parents needed a countermeasure to life in Haldeman. The majority of fans used cons as a replacement for an absent family, and my parents did the same. They preferred cons to their children's high school and college graduations, or my sister's appearance on the homecoming court. On one occasion Dad returned from a con proud of having cried in public because he felt comfortable among his "family." I believe that telling his children this was an attempt to communicate that he was capable of weeping, despite never doing so in front of us. But what came across was the notion that fans were more deserving of his emotional vulnerability than we were.

Dad seldom left the house over which he held utter dominion. When he did leave, he went to cons, an environment that assuaged his ego in every way. He grew accustomed to these two extremes and became resentful when his family failed to treat him like fans did. We disappointed him with our need for a father.

Chapter Twenty-six

WITH JOHN Cleve in official retirement, Turk Winter surged forth as my father's last persona, publishing more than 250 titles. Dad referred to him as "a perverse, kinky devil born for one book; reinpsychelated in 1975." Before his final trip to New York, Dad had written a fan letter to Eric Stanton, an underground fetish artist who drew *On a Kinky Hook*. Dad thought he'd recognized the artistic influence of Steve Ditko, the mysterious genius who created Spider-Man and Dr. Strange. Stanton responded with an appreciative phone call. Impressed by Dad's visual sense, he explained that Ditko had been his studio mate for several years. They talked for an hour, and Stanton invited Dad to visit on his business trip to Manhattan.

Expecting the worst sort of rudeness from a native New Yorker, Dad was shocked by Stanton's hospitality: private sleeping quarters stocked with whiskey and porn. Though they were from drastically different backgrounds—Stanton was a Brooklyn native who'd served in the navy—they had much in common. Dad used pseudonyms and Stanton had legally changed his name from Ernest

Stanzoni. As boys, they'd both copied pages from *Kaanga,* a comic book that featured light bondage. They loved the 1940s matinee serial *Perils of Nyoka.* Their initial meeting was similar to a pair of immigrants from the Old Country discovering each other, assuaging loneliness by speaking the same language: corset and heels, rope and strap, whip and cane.

Stanton's art and Dad's prose were heavily influenced by a particular type of comic called a "bondage serial," consisting of a narrative with words and art, sold through the mail a single page at a time. According to Dad's papers, in 1952 he encountered an ad in the back of a men's magazine for *Princess Elaine's Terrible Fate,* drawn by Gene Bilbrew. Dad bought a full set, his first exposure to bondage art. He then contracted with Bizarre Inc. to create his own serial, corresponding with an editor who signed letters as "Sado Mazie." Dad wrote and drew ten chapters. It was rejected for amateurish art, but the writing was good enough that Sado Mazie offered to swap merchandise for scripts. Insulted, Dad refused. Seven years later he tried again, submitting work to publisher Irving Klaw, and again he was rejected.

My father was astounded that Stanton knew Bilbrew and Klaw personally. Stanton was equally amazed by Dad's encyclopedic knowledge of the fetish field. They decided to collaborate. There was no business arrangement, no legal contract, no formal division of profits and labor. They operated under an old-fashioned gentlemen's agreement. This was partly to avoid prosecution but was also a product of their generation—they simply decided to trust each other. Stanton paid for printing and distribution in exchange for retaining all copyrights. Dad's payment came in the form of free porn. They collaborated for twenty-five years, the longest time either man had a business partner.

There existed a sense of play in their collaboration, that of teen-agers engaged in naughty behavior, delighting in the other's con-tributions. Their methodology was simple. Stanton mailed Dad a sheaf of drawings photocopied from his sketchbook. After shuffling the sequence of art, Dad inserted dialogue, blocks of text, and ideas for trimming or lengthening the story. He mailed the pages back to Stanton, who called Dad to discuss. They talked as often as twice a week, both men drinking and laughing, telling stories and planning their future work.

The concept of warrior women appealed to them, which led to the creation of their popular series *Blunder Broad,* a parody of Wonder Woman. She battled aliens and supervillains such as Count Dastardly, Pussygirl, and Doktor Weerde. Every story ended with her capture, often bound by her own lasso. They also created a series about "princkazons," Amazonian women with penises—essentially large-breasted transsexuals who dominated males and females alike. Dad used the name Turk Winter for all their collab-orative work.

Their few nonprofessional letters had a jocular tone, filled with juvenile sex jokes and humorous comments. They made fun of each other's accents, where they lived, and fetish preferences. If one didn't respond in a timely manner, he was accused of "cock-teasing" the other. Reading these letters made me glad that my father had someone with whom he could loosen up and relinquish his mar-tinet qualities. Despite having spent very little time with Stanton, Dad always referred to Eric as his best friend. I wondered if it was true until I found a note from one of Stanton's adult children refer-ring to Dad as Eric's best friend.

Dad wrote faster than Stanton drew, and began his own self-publishing imprint called Winterbooks. Stanton promoted the material to his mail-order clients. Customers initially went through

Stanton, which delayed fulfillment of the orders. As the volume increased, Dad began dealing directly with repeat clients. He developed a list of offerings and charged sixty dollars per book, payable in advance. In this way, both men made money by selling the same material to different customers.

By 1999 Stanton had endured a series of strokes that rendered him unable to work. He gave Dad an extensive list of American and international clients. Eric Stanton died on April 17, 1999. That same day, Dad suffered a massive heart attack, requiring emergency bypass surgery. The death of his only friend left him alone with his obsessions.

Two years after heart surgery, my father expanded Winterbooks, referring to it as "Turk's cottage industry." Dad sent personal letters to big spenders, alluding to porn he custom-wrote for special clients. A slow-going epistolary relationship developed in which Dad gave them gifts, confided personal details, and hinted at his actual name. Like a clandestine agent operating under a cloak of secrecy, he revealed himself to men he could exploit financially. Over time several customers specified their sadomasochistic interests and ordered their own private pornography. The price was three thousand dollars, but each customer was offered a "special discount" that dropped the rate to $2,600. If a customer paid cash in advance, Dad wrote the tailor-made porn.

He fed the prose into a computer template he'd invented for a seventy-page book—two vertical columns of text. The final product was a manuscript with a special cover page personally inscribed, dated, and signed by Turk Winter. Dad later changed the cover page and added the commissioned work to his catalog, reselling each one for seventy dollars, unsigned. This had the unexpected effect of pleasing the original clients, who enjoyed the notion of like-minded strangers reading a professional depiction of their personal fantasies. Within ten years Dad had a large catalog of books for sale, eking out a living while proudly continuing the underground tradition of mail-order bondage begun in the 1940s.

Customers in the UK, Germany, and Italy routinely requested swifter ordering, suggesting fax or email, and a method of payment other than cash. One went so far as providing his credit card number. Dad refused, trusting nobody, especially the Internet. Obscenity laws were relegated to local standards, and he lived deep in the Bible Belt. Using the postal system to defraud the IRS was a felony, and Dad received bundles of cash in the mail on a regular basis. As protection, he mailed Winterbooks from the post office in Morehead, which sent packages to Lexington for a postmark, placing a hundred-mile layer of discretion between him and their official source. He used false return addresses, including mine. While living in Montana, I received a tattered envelope from Italy that contained a manuscript the customer didn't want, along with a letter in stilted English explaining its return.

Dad maintained steady correspondence with repeat customers. He saved their letters but not his own. This resulted in files going back over a decade that contained one side of a continuous conversation. I read hundreds, slowly seeing a pattern emerge of characteristics shared by most of the men: over forty, middle-class to wealthy, many with a Catholic childhood. They worked as civil servants, lawyers, and middle managers in corporate offices. American clients often had backgrounds in the military or engineering. All were incredibly lonely, having carried around their secret obsession without a chance to share it. The letters reminded me of film buffs or musicologists who established credentials by displaying the depth of their knowledge. Most hobbyists have meeting places such as a record store, a gun show, or a philatelist's event. There they are free to bask in a shared interest. But a bird-watcher doesn't have to hide his binoculars the way bondage enthusiasts conceal everything related to their hobby.

Clients treated Turk Winter with great respect. The more money they spent, the longer Turk's letters were. With men of his own generation, Dad discussed health issues between paragraphs concerned with bondage and discipline. They exchanged VHS tapes, magazines, and photocopies of underground art.

Long-term pen pals included information about new cars, broken appliances, the weather, and popular movies. At least two thanked my father for photographs of his children and grandchildren. Instead of communicating with his family, Dad preferred an ongoing correspondence with people he never met. The mutual interest in bondage material was a powerful link, ingrained with sympathy and understanding. After carrying his secret throughout his life, he could be himself with strangers.

Since childhood, Dad had felt ashamed of his sexual proclivities. He knew they were unusual, possible evidence of something fundamentally flawed with his mind. This sense of difference resulted in an extreme degree of loneliness that was reduced by writing letters. One fan letter closed with a few lines that echoed a long-held belief of Dad's: "Your stories allow our minds to be satiated without committing unspeakable acts. They keep us 'civilized' and sane. Maybe you have not heard it from others but it's true."

In the course of his fifty-year career as a writer, my father explored every sexual permutation except pedophilia. At the end of his life, still seeking a frontier, he wrote an intricate portrayal of cannibalism. His sole foray into bestiality was combined with the medical cloning of goats. In 2011 Turk Winter completed his final two serials. *Gurlz* encompassed nine installments for a total of 675 pages. *Barbi's World* was over a thousand pages long. Stacked beside his chair were sheets of paper that contained his last writings: a list of real and invented nouns, and a succinct summary for a new book. My father was a workhorse in the field of written pornography. After five decades he died in harness.

Chapter Twenty-seven

MY FATHER'S writing process was simple—he got an idea, brainstormed a few notes, then wrote the first chapter. Next he developed an outline from one to ten pages long. He followed the outline carefully, relying on it to dictate the narrative. He composed his first drafts longhand, wearing rubber thimbles on finger and thumb. Writing with a felt-tip pen, he produced thirty or forty pages in a sitting. Upon completion of a full draft, he transcribed the material with his typewriter, revising as he went. Most writers get more words per page as they go from longhand to a typed manuscript, but not Dad. His handwriting was small and he used abbreviations. His first drafts were often the same length as the final ones.

Manuscripts of science fiction and heroic fantasy received multiple revisions, but he had to work much faster on porn. After a handwritten first chapter, he typed the rest swiftly, made editorial changes, and passed that draft to my mother. She retyped it for final submission. Under financial pressure, Mom would be typing the beginning of the book while Dad was writing the end. His goal was a minimum of a book a month. To achieve that, he refined his methods further.

Industrial mass production is based on efficiency and speed. Faced with increasing demand, Dad invented a method that enabled him to maintain supply with a minimum of effort. He created batches of raw material in advance—phrases, sentences, descriptions, and entire scenes on hundreds of pages organized in three-ring binders. Tabbed index dividers separated the sections into topics.

Dad was like Henry Ford applying principles of assembly-line production with premade parts. The methodical technique proved highly efficient. Surrounded by his tabulated notebooks, he could quickly find the appropriate section and transcribe lines directly into his manuscript. Afterward, he blacked them out to prevent plagiarizing himself. Ford hired a team of workers to manufacture a Model T in six hours. Working alone, Dad could write a book in three days.

Eighty percent of the notebooks described aspects of women's bodies. The longest section focused on their bosom. Here is a brief compendium.

BREASTS:

love-swollen little buds
nascent curves
quivering mound
gentle hillox of her acorn-shaped brsts
tight hard mounds w/pointed crests
tender curve of her half-ripe breasts
firm and tight-skinned as new pears dangling unpicked
    from sun-warmed trees

gleamed w/the bloom of ripe peaches—w/same firmness
thrusting artillery shells
cannister jutted
opulently jutting projections
slick-skinned titty curves
meaty pendants
cantilevered coneshapes
unnatural thrust of those conoid mounds
bulging sides of her shapely creamballs
loosely attached knockers swayed from her chest
unbelieveable pulchritude of her overripe balls
big hard bullets of brazenly firm flesh

Another binder listed descriptions of individual actions, separated by labeling tabs that included: Mouth. Tongue. Face. Legs. Kiss. The heading of Orgasm had subdivisions of before, during, and after. The section called entry received the most precision, with subheadings of Virginal, Anal, Vaginal, Standing, Oral, and Kneeling. The thickest notebook, designed strictly for BDSM novels, listed of 150 synonyms for "pain." Sections included spanking, whipping, degradation, pre-degradation, distress, screams, restraints, and tortures. These were further subdivided into specific categories followed by brief descriptions of each.

One long section gave me serious concern—a twenty page document titled *Notes for a Book on Cruelty: Man's Oldest Pleasure*—a succinct list of tortures used throughout history in twelve countries. Examples included the partial flaying of people, insertion of bugs and rodents into fresh stomach wounds, nailing objects through flesh into bones, legs masoned into walls, the dislocation of arms, and cutting away various body parts. All were legal punishments mandated by the courts or society. The majority ended in slow, painful death. One source was a long diary recorded by a professional torturer of suspected witches in 1621.

1) Woman bound on rack,
2) Poured oil over head and burned,
3) Placed sulphur in armpits, burned it,
4) Hands tied behind, hauled up to ceiling, dropped,
5) Torturer went to lunch,
6) Placed spiked board on her back, pulled to ceiling, dropped,
7) Toes pressed in thumbscrews until blood squirted,
8) Pinched with red-hot irons,
9) Whipped and put in vise, gradually closed for six hours,
10) Hung by thumbs and flogged.
"This was all that was done on the first day."

The final sentence chilled me. My impulse was to skip over the material completely, but I couldn't shy away due to my own distaste. Instead, I tried to understand. My father had read dozens of books, copied sections in longhand, then organized his notes into a chronicle of terrible human activity. It was not scholarship on his part; he didn't seek the information in order to place it in a larger context to further human knowledge. At first I suspected Dad sought inspiration, but none of his own books included the specific techniques he'd compiled. It occurred to me that he was using history to justify his own obsessive interest, seeking precedent to indulge his fantasies. For thousands of years people have treated other people in a horrible manner. Humans systematically tortured one another for political, social, and religious reasons. Someone performed all these acts, and someone else made a record for posterity. My father's imagined worlds were nothing compared to historic reality.

Later my mother called and invited me to watch her beloved Reds play the Cardinals. I went to her house, grateful for the respite. It was a short drive through the lovely landscape of northern Mississippi, the thick foliage heavy with green. The sky was violet at dusk. The road to Oxford dipped and a church came into view. Briefly I had the sensation I was in Kentucky, driving to Haldeman to visit my mother.

At Mom's house we spent twenty minutes fiddling with the television remote control and discovered that the Reds game was blacked out locally. Mom found a cop show she liked, then muted the volume and asked how work was going on the book.

I laughed and said, "Porn, porn, porn."

She told me about taking a box of pornography to science fiction conventions and selling the books to fans.

"They bought them," she said. "They bought everything. I don't know why. The books were pretty much all the same. Different settings and people's names, but the same. People just like them, I guess."

"It's like Agatha Christie novels. Or TV shows. A satisfying formula."

"With sex," she said, and laughed.

I told her I'd found a notebook with scads of notes about torture. The extensiveness of the material surprised me.

"It shouldn't," she said. "Your father was interested in that, you know."

"What did you think of that?"

"It was historical." She shrugged slightly. "He had a lot of interests. Like you do. Remember when you did that magic show at the library? You had a lot of hobbies."

She was right, I had many hobbies as a child, and at one time wanted to be a stage magician. Maybe Dad's study of torture was similar, a short-term enthusiasm.

"Whenever I talk about Dad's career," I said, "people always ask about your sex life."

"Whose?"

"Yours."

"Why would they want to know that?"

"I guess because of the porn," I said.

"What do you tell them?" she said.

"I say it's not something we discuss."

She thought for a moment, then spoke. "Tell them it's none of their damn business."

"Okay, Mom."

We turned our attention to the silent flickering on the television. The lead actor presided over a team, and Mom explained each of the specialist roles: fighter, tech, rookie, weaponry. The sound was unnecessary. I could see the characters surrounding a floor plan and planning an assault. They walked through a house with guns and flashlights, then chased a shirtless man in a car. I knew the car would wreck and they'd arrest the driver, and I knew the team would later capture the real bad guy, the boss of the shirtless man. A predictable formula satisfied the viewers, the same as it did for readers of Dad's porn.

Mom told me she was content, that she liked living alone, and wondered if she should feel guilty about that.

"Do you?" I said.

"No, but I think I should."

"You're eighty, Mom. You deserve a break. No need to feel guilty about having a life you like."

"You know," she said, "you're right."

"Do you ever miss him?"

"Not really. Sometimes watching TV at night. Somebody to talk to."

"Well, I'm here." I pointed to the silent television set. "Good show, huh?" I said.

We both laughed. Later I hugged her, setting off the high-pitched keening of her hearing aid, and said goodbye.

I drove home and watched thousands of lightning bugs float in a field against the dark tree line. Cicadas roared steadily. The sound of frogs rose and fell. A whip-poor-will called, then a barred owl. Despite the beauty of the night, I could not rid myself of the tortures my father had compiled.

Chapter Twenty-eight

MONTHS OF close proximity to my father's pattern of thought influenced me to think like him, then behave like him—distant, preoccupied, and critical. I began to question myself, the validity of my undertaking. At times my mood veered into self-hatred. I wasn't suicidal, but the notion flitted through my mind, an option hiding in the shadowy perimeter. It concerned me enough to take a break from Dad's papers.

I thought of the poet John Berryman, whose father killed himself, an act from which no son could ever recover. In a poem called "Of Suicide," he wrote:

> *Reflexions on suicide, & on my father, possess me.*
> *I drink too much.*

I first read this poem in my early twenties with little knowledge about Berryman, having heard incorrectly that he had leaped to his death from the Golden Gate Bridge. The poem had an exotic appeal, a glamorization of suicide and liquor. The lines were meaningful to me, since I often felt possessed by thoughts of my father and his occasional talk of suicide.

A few years after reading the poem, I happened to be in Minneapolis. A friend took me to the bleak Washington Avenue Bridge and pointed out the spot—not where Berryman jumped but where he landed—on the bank of the Mississippi River. It was a shocking moment for me, destroying the romantic notion of the bearded genius soaring from the grand and misty Golden Gate into the sea. Instead, in the middle of a brutal midwestern winter, he jumped off an ugly narrow bridge and died from the impact with frozen dirt.

The last time I lived in Kentucky, my house sat on a hill overlooking a pond, and in the morning the birds declared their various overlapping territories while snatching insects near the surface of the water. I often rose early to listen to them, then returned to bed. Before moving away, I placed a cheap cassette recorder outside and recorded the birds. For many years I carried the tape as a last resort to homesickness. If despair overran me, the knowledge that I could listen to the birds provided strength. The cassette was similar to the Robert Arthur short story "Mr. Manning's Money Tree," in which the promise of cash buried beneath a tree sustains a man through difficult financial times. Knowledge of its existence allows him to take business risks he might have avoided. At the end he digs up the money, but it's not there.

I decided to listen to the tape, surrounded by my father's dusty archives. It seemed appropriate to hear Kentucky birdsong amid all this material made in Haldeman. The cassette emitted a series of clicks followed by a continual hum. There was no birdsong. Years before, I'd pressed the wrong buttons on the recording device. Like the buried money of Mr. Manning, the promise of hearing the birds when I needed them had gotten me through hard times. The absurdity of the situation cheered me.

Many years ago I purchased an original painting by Ronald Cooper, a Kentucky folk artist of some repute. The eleven-by-fourteen painting is acrylic on canvas. An unpainted section on the bottom right corner has the date 1994, a copyright sign, the artist's signature, and the name of the painting: *Suicide*. The colors are straight from the tube, unmixed, and the drawing is quite crude. The composition is divided in half—the top is a blue background strung with clouds, while the bottom is a field of solid green. In the foreground stands a man wearing a black shirt and white pants. Spots of blood mar his clothes. Protruding from his shirt collar is the stump of a bleeding neck. He grips a bloody butcher knife in one hand, while the other holds aloft his own decapitated head. An arrow beside his mouth points to the words:

i WiSH i HADNT DONE THiS.

I kept the painting hidden, believing it was too gruesome for my young sons to see. When they got older, I hung it in my writing studio and imagined it as the cover for a book. The face of the bleeding head has an expression of startled dismay, as if he can't quite accept his situation. I believe I'd feel the same way if I killed myself—stunned regret at the final millisecond, too late to turn back. It reminds me of the legends of the French guillotine: a freshly cut-off head blinking in a basket, the mouth struggling to speak, the body unwilling to accept its own death.

Like anyone, I suppose, I have known several people who killed themselves, including my best friend from childhood. Such a death leaves guilt in its wake. Every surviving friend and family member believes that he or she could have prevented it. Each person recalls a visit not made or a phone call cut short. We pore over our final interactions, seeking a retrospective portent of the future that came to be. We want a sign that it was not our fault.

I look at the painting now and wonder why it commanded my attention for so long. It's an ugly thing made with brute force, the crude style echoing the figure's dilemma. What began as a personal warning—don't kill yourself—has evolved into a commentary about the nature of remorse. The man has a deep regret: *I wish I hadn't done this.*

Twice in my life I experienced what I understood to be severe depression. Every action was unimaginable: getting the mail, rising from a chair, making the bed, taking a shower. The act of concocting my own extinction would be too much effort. Then there'd be the burden of the note left behind. Where to start and where to end? I tend to get depressed if I'm not engaged in a writing project, and it seemed supremely depressing that revising a suicide note might rescue me from the doldrums. Despite my fascination with the painting, I am not by nature suicidal. I have more of a gambler's mentality—everything can change at any moment, so why make a move with such undeniable finality?

In 1985 I received a strange phone call from my parents, both on the line at once, expressing concern for my mental health and possible suicide. I was astonished and laughed it off until I understood that they were serious. There followed a flurry of calls over several days during which my parents retreated from their initial concerns and blamed my sister for putting the idea in their heads. My mother sent me a letter that said:

> *I don't and didn't think for one minute that you were in danger of contemplating suicide. You're too curious about life, and are too afraid you might miss something to take your dying into your own hands. Therefore*

you would not take your own life. It was your father's
runaway imagination that produced the concern for
you.

  Not long ago I bought some new makeup, including
rouge. Two weeks later Andy said he wanted to ask me
something, very seriously. He was worried that something
had happened to my face, one of my cheeks was
discolored. No, it was the rouge and he waited two weeks
before bringing it up.

  Runaway imagination. Always looking for some
complicated, dramatic reason instead of thinking of the
simple. Surely you can understand that, since if anybody
inherited the runaway imagination, you did.

I enjoy Mom's positive spin on a grotesque situation, utilizing a certain cold logic to reach her conclusion. The succinctness of her anecdote, the blunt reasoning, reminds me that I am her son as well, half McCabe—pragmatic people who stare clear-eyed at obstacles and overcome them. My imagination is tempered by reason, grounded in harsh reality.

A few years later Dad began calling me late at night, maudlin from bourbon. He said he'd been thinking about suicide. He'd even picked out the place—the bathroom shower—so it'd be easy for Mom to clean the mess. He figured he'd use a shotgun but had run into a problem. His arms were too short to reach the trigger. My first thought was practical: *use a forked stick.* But I refrained from advice, and merely listened. He believed that putting the barrel against the roof of his mouth instead of his forehead would ensure success because the tissue was very soft. I said that made sense, thinking not about my father but about a buddy who'd shot himself in the temple with a small-caliber handgun. The bullet hit the skull and deflected, losing power from impact. Instead of ricocheting away, the bullet traveled around the front of his forehead below his skin. He lived, badly scarred and partially deaf. Another guy I knew deliberately rammed his car head-on into a coal truck at high speed, but only managed to blind himself. Three other friends had gotten the job done, so it was with a certain hardened ear that I listened to my father.

I wasn't sure if he was serious or operating within delusion; for all I knew, I was talking to John Cleve. The last time he'd called drunk, he'd been in an exhilarated state, claiming he could fly. I told him that was great, he could come visit. "No," he explained, "I mean really fly. I stand at the head of the steps and absolutely know if I jump, I will fly to the downstairs hall." Presumably he never tried it.

At the end of that suicide call, the first of many, I asked if he'd talked to Mom about this and he got angry, saying *of course not* in a familiar tone of contempt. The following day I called Mom and told her to unload the shotgun. She didn't ask why. For the last twenty-five years I lived with the understanding that at any moment I might receive the news that Dad had killed himself. I wondered where the family would bathe when we gathered for his death. As the oldest, I'd have to use the shower first. To prepare myself, I imagined the act in great detail, down to my own post-traumatic hallucination of seeing the soapsuds run pink from traces of blood embedded in the grout.

After he died, I found the old shotgun hanging on hooks above a door, the metal pitted, the action rusty, the barrel filled with grime. It was a break-action single-barrel .410, forty-two inches long. I placed the barrel against my face and could easily reach the trigger. Dad was taller, with much longer arms than mine. Either he'd lied to me on the phone or he'd traded in a twelve-gauge for one with a shorter barrel.

The .410 was ideal for snake, and I brought it back to Mississippi. A pack of coyotes travels a wide territory here, showing up every few weeks and disturbing my wife's dogs with their chilling howls. Firing the old .410 makes enough noise to send the coyotes elsewhere. Every time I shoot, I think of my father's dismal talk of suicide, and how he drank himself to death while the shotgun rusted on the wall.

Chapter Twenty-nine

DURING THE heart of Mississippi winter, I missed the purity of fresh snow but not the northern cold. Still, the days were short, with gray skies and a barren tree line. My house lacked insulation. The pipes froze. Fetishized sex became a white noise that surrounded me, invading every aspect of my life. In order to interact objectively with porn, I had to deliberately repress any salacious response to the material, which was like going to a comedy club and trying not to laugh. Months of immersion in pornography had reversed its intended purpose. Instead of arousal, I became sexually numb. I didn't even want to be touched. Marital relations waned, ebbed, and vanished. I felt guilty.

My life consisted of a house full of porn and a gorgeous wife—but the two were unconnected. I became afraid my wife would go elsewhere for sex, seek a man who'd inherited money and land instead of mountains of porn. She said that was crazy talk, suggesting my disinterest was a normal product of grief. But I didn't feel grief. I'd developed an immunity to sex. I was sick of my involvement with porn. I'd become a useless steer. My wife wouldn't have to leave. The young bulls would trample me into the mud and take her away.

In *A Clockwork Orange* by Anthony Burgess, the protagonist is subjected to a form of aversion therapy. His eyelids are clipped open by specula, then he's forced to watch brutally violent images until he is rendered incapable of harming others. My experience was similar. I'd forced myself to interact with so much pornography, I no longer regarded my wife in a sexual manner. Each time I tried, my mind filled with images of fetish porn. I could admire her dress, legs and hips, but the response was aesthetic and intellectual, as if studying art I couldn't afford.

I got worried and saw a doctor. He inquired if I had erections at night or in the morning. I nodded, embarrassed. In a light, jocular tone, he said it wasn't the equipment, so there was no need for Viagra. I tried to force a smile that fell apart before reaching my face. The doctor asked if my wife was undergoing menopause, and he seemed slightly surprised that she was younger, as if her age alone should keep me sexually engaged.

In a subtle fashion, he probed about my professional life. After hearing a brief explanation of my current project, the doctor quickly changed the subject to my deviated septum, which affected my breathing. He said the extreme degree of trauma was common in adults who'd had their nose broken in childhood and never repaired. He gently asked if I'd ever been hit in the face as a kid. For the first time in weeks, I started laughing. Of course, I told him, hasn't everybody? He gave me a strange look and sent me home. Later it occurred to me that in its own way, porn had struck me as hard as the blow that shattered cartilage inside my head. I feared that my desire, like my ability to breathe normally, would never return.

People with eating disorders maintain distorted thinking that leads them to deny themselves food. The malady is cognitive, not organic, which means drugs don't help; patients must reframe their thinking to make food palatable. I needed to do the same with sex but didn't know how. I considered burning everything page by page, watching each piece of paper curl, igniting at the edges, flaring into quick yellow flame that would provide kindling for the next lurid depiction of sex. But I couldn't light the match. Burning it would take hours. Most grandiose gestures are suspect—the couple who renew their vows just before divorce or the politician who publicly swears he's clean, then enters rehab. Building a pyre of porn wouldn't guarantee an automatic return of desire. I'd just regret it later.

The winter solstice clamped its lid on the earth. January's chill led to weeks of short gray days with morning frost heavy enough to track a rabbit. Our home had high ceilings and a furnace designed for a smaller structure. At night I built a massive fire, effectively sucking warmth from the house but heating a small area before the hearth. My wife and I pushed the furniture near the fireplace and sat beneath wool blankets. During the day I shuffled about, shifting porn into ever-expanding heaps. Like my father, I'd transformed the entire house into a workstation devoted to the same material. In a lifetime of struggle not to feel bad about myself, I'd never felt worse. The future appeared bleak. I was a failure on all fronts.

Spring arrived in fits and starts. Each time I thought I'd built the last fire and resolved to cut my hair and shave my beard, cold weather declared its intentions. A woodpecker drilled a hole in the exterior wall. Two starlings used the hole for an entrance and built a nest inside. One morning I awoke early to the sound of young birds frantically calling from the walls of the house.

I stepped outside to watch ground fog lifting from the back field. Six deer browsed the yellow sedge grass. A flash of movement caught my eye—a fox pouncing on prey at the field's edge. The deer froze in place. The fox turned with a vole dangling from its mouth and trotted into the herd, then halted. The deer were immobile, tails cocked, poised to flee. The fox slowly turned its head from one deer to another, then moved on, vanishing into the woods. The deer returned to their feeding. The animals had assessed each other, found a lack of danger, and continued their lives.

I continued to work, make fires at night, and write. The days warmed slowly, becoming longer, with more light. My libido returned like snow leaving a metal roof—the slight breaking of its icy surface, then the sudden cascade as the entire mass swept itself clean, the steep-pitched slope gleaming in the sun as if it had always been that way.

Chapter Thirty

AS CHILDREN, my siblings and I each had a box of sixty-four Crayola crayons. They were special crayons, a gift from our father, along with high-quality coloring books he ordered by mail. Dad had his own set. After supper the family often sat at the table and colored together. Dad carefully read the name of each crayon before using it, explaining that he was partially color-blind. Soon we stepped up to sophisticated coloring books with more intricate designs, using felt-tip pens that we stored in cigar boxes. As we got older, we colored less often, until at some point we stopped altogether. Those evenings remain my best memories of family life.

After Dad's death, I found hundreds of dried and useless felt-tip pens from various drawers of his desk. Each pen held a slip of paper taped to the shaft that identified the color, similar to the label on a crayon. I filled a box with eighty folders of original art. In Mississippi I opened that box and made my final significant discovery. Behind my father's public identity as a science fiction writer and his covert life as a pornographer was yet another private enterprise.

For over fifty years, he secretly made comic books of a sexual nature and neatly filed them away.

The first item in each file was something innocuous—a Reds schedule or an old bill—as if concealing the true contents. No one entered his office except by invitation, and even then, none dared go behind his desk. His children had been out of the house more than twenty-five years. Concealment was part of his creative process, born of shame and guilt, which he maintained long after there was anyone to hide it from. He needed the fetish of secrecy in order to draw.

My father never took an art class. He didn't visit museums or draw from a model. He'd taught himself from studying comic books, illustrations in pulp magazines, and bondage serials from the forties and fifties. Scenes lacked perspective, and the anatomy was crude. His earliest work is reminiscent of Henry Darger's drawings, based on imagination rather than observation. When Dad began drawing as a child, he didn't comprehend female anatomy, and for a long time he believed the vagina was in the middle of the stomach because babies came from there. He didn't know women had pubic hair.

Frustrated by his lack of skill, he developed a complicated and time-consuming way of making comics. First he wrote a script that described the action. On separate pages he made loose pencil layouts of panels. He fed the layouts into his typewriter and carefully typed segments of narrative into the allotted areas. After removing the paper, he used the typed sections as guides for what to draw.

Dad called his method of drawing "the steal technique." He traced images from other works, transferred the tracing to a second page via carbon paper, and modified them by enlarging sexual characteristics. Then he inked and colored the pages. Dad believed that he enhanced any picture he stole due to an innate ability to improve everyone else's work. A dozen thick notebooks held thousands of pages of source material, images torn from magazines and catalogs, divided by category: standing, sitting, sex, breasts, legs, and so forth. He dismantled hundreds of porn magazines to accumulate a reservoir of pictures to steal. Mixed in were images from lingerie catalogs, *Heavy Metal* magazine, and *Entertainment Weekly*.

As a very young child, I had a Superman coloring book my father had given me. I colored every page that featured Superman, which left the scenes of Clark Kent interacting with other characters. These were very boring, since everyone wore office attire, and I began coloring the suits brightly with different hues for the lapels and pockets. While concentrating, I realized that my father stood behind me, watching with an intense frown. He asked why I colored that way. Instantly I understood it was wrong. "I got tired of blue," I said, and wished I hadn't, since he was wearing a blue suit. He didn't answer, just looked away, thinking for a long time. Many years later Dad asked if I remembered the incident and I told him yes.

"Me, too," he said. "You taught me something then. There are no rules for coloring."

He'd inherited deuteranopia, a form of color-blindness that affected his perception of the green-yellow-red section of the spectrum. This genetic flaw bothered him throughout his life. To avoid clashing colors, he wore dark clothes. The lack of rules for coloring freed him from the pressure of making a mistake. Blending color for subtlety was impossible with felt-tip pens. Most of the figures in his comics were unclothed, their skin blue or green. The hues were bright and flat. His lack of facility with color produced lurid and shocking, unusual combinations matching the intensity of the scenes.

Along with the comics was a personal document dated 1963,

with the caveat that it be read after his death. He was twenty-nine when he wrote it. I was five. It was his only sustained example of personal writing. He referred to the comics as his "Great Secret" and revealed a deep concern about his zeal for the material. He worried that he hated women. He wondered if there were other people like him and, if so, how they dealt with their urges.

At age fourteen, he'd begun drawing comics that portrayed women in torment, before he'd had any exposure to fetish material or knowledge of sadism. The impulse was simply inside him; he'd always been that way. He called his comics an atrocity. The locked box in which he kept them was "full of my shame and my wickedness and my weakness."

The document has a sincere quality absent in everything else he wrote. Without his usual grandiosity, the intent probing of his own psyche makes him vulnerable enough for sympathy.

> *I have wasted hundreds of hours at this, always fearful of discovery, always secretive, always aware of the sickness and hating myself for it. I well know the utter dream-fiction stupidity of it, even while continuing through page after gory, naked page after blood-splashed page, after ordeal-filled page. I know it's silly, tom-foolery. And I'm ashamed: I know it's sick.*
>
> *I'm sorry, sorry. Who is to blame? It can only be my childhood . . . because these things took place in it, after certain patterns were formed, after certain circuitry was already branded on my mental relays. Mother, Dad, Judeo-Christianity, and my childhood friends.*
>
> *It is the repressions, not the manifestations of unrepressed thoughts, that give us trouble. Apparently I am giving them vent, egress, by drawing page after page.*
>
> *But what if I stop?*

In 1957, just before getting married, he packed a decade's worth of his art in a sack with rocks and threw it into the Cumberland River. He wrote that no one knew what it had taken for him to do that. He swore never to make such material again. Eighteen months later, he began *The Saga of Valkyria Barbosa* and worked on it for the rest of his life. It ran one hundred and twenty separate books that totaled four thousand pages.

As a lonely teenager in a log cabin, he'd invented the premise: a barbarian culture crossed with the highly advanced science of Atlantis. Aging was medically quickened to bypass childhood. Breasts were enlarged with special serums and could lactate and grow upon command. Subcutaneous skin dye replaced clothing. The healing process was hastened, with no infection or scars. The dead could be resurrected. Hymens were restored. The only permanent disfigurement came from branding and amputation.

The protagonist, Valkyria, was a barbarian princess secretly raised as a boy, later trained as a warrior. She was kidnapped by desert raiders, sold to slavers, purchased by a wealthy merchant, and kidnapped again by pirates. At age nineteen, she became queen of Veltria. Nearly all the characters were female, with the exception of an occasional hermaphrodite. According to Dad's notes, the pictorial domination of women by women was a practical decision—he preferred to draw them.

The concept of a universe was too limiting for his imagination, and he created a complex multiverse in which all the comics took place. The multiple worlds of *Valkyria* were staggeringly complicated, with Dad's trademark maps, glossary, and religions. The entire series was a never-ending narrative set on many planets, spanning thousands of years. It blended fairy tales, ancient legends, science fiction, and space opera into one sprawling story.

The books had no audience, but the first and last pages were composed as if a preexisting readership eagerly awaited the next installment. Every comic ended with the phrase "to be continued." The first page featured a single-panel illustration and a quick synopsis:

> *This is the fabulous myth-history of the pre-recorded history heroine, Valkyria. A girl with a face and figure envied by temptresses . . . The cunning, the speed, the agility of a jungle cat . . . The muscles, the stamina, the fighting prowess of a professional soldier.*
>
> *Val's wounds heal themselves, scarlessly, even monstrously serious ones. Unfortunately this form of indestructible immortality makes her the perfect victim!*

In order to combine all the worlds and time frames into a single overlapping narrative, Dad gave Valkyria several daughters, each born of rape. The infants received serums from Atlantean science that sped their growth. Within three months they reached puberty and were again injected. Their final growth spurt enhanced their sexual characteristics and halted their aging at eighteen. By age twenty-two, Valkyria had become a grandmother. "Real time" was thus collapsed, enabling each of these women to travel across the multiverse until captured, tortured, and rescued.

The plot is similar from book to book: a highborn woman is brought down through systematic psychological humiliation and physical degradation. The motivation for torture is always vengeance—the victim deserves her fate. Melodramatic dialogue offsets the grim imagery. Each comic ends with a cliff-hanger of inescapable bondage in a secret dungeon. The next book prolongs the torture until the victim is rescued or escapes, whereupon she often turns the tables on the captor. Of necessity, the punishment must surpass the one endured by the previous victim. In this fashion the techniques of sexual suffering steadily increase in intensity and horror. The bondage becomes more complex—victims are fully immobilized, with every orifice plugged, while enduring elaborate sexual torture. At times Valkyria is compelled to watch her daughters undergo vicious assault.

The relentless narrative has a grotesque quality, a chilling insight into the mind of a man with an unsavory attitude toward women. They undergo brain transplants and watch their former bodies die in an acid bath. Hermaphrodites fight warrior women wearing strap-on dildos with metal claws. Zombies, androids, and clones enter the narrative. A snake crawls into a woman's vagina, swelling her stomach with pregnancy. She gives birth to a demon who promptly rapes her.

In a book from the mid-1960s, Valkyria travels through time to the year 2931. Her clone becomes a media star when a TV network shows her torment on a live feed. Viewers respond to a contest with ideas. The lucky winner visits the studio and is allowed to personally torture Valkyria's clone to death. In an off-camera dungeon, the true Valkyria experiences every sensation. The reader is thus able to observe the suffering of both clone and human.

One volume of *Valkyria* centers around an alien scientist who performs gruesome medical experiments on humans, often depicting surgeries in process. The result is a planet populated by failed procedures: women with a single large breast centered on their chests. A mustached man has a woman's backside, large breasts, and an enormous permanent erection. Women have two or three sets of breasts linked by metal rings. A green-skinned transsexual has three breasts and a large clitoris shaped like a penis. The scientist is presented as: "The most brilliant man on this planet. He has a short attention span and more ideas than he can handle; is essentially amoral (he is nigh a god!) and does believe in giving in to his whims. He looks upon the world as his."

Another comic, *Prisma,* is less a book and more of an illustrated manifesto. It is the only one narrated in the first person. The sadistic tinkerer Volk is the most brilliant scientist who ever existed. He explains his project with many detailed illustrations.

> *I made 10 androids, perfect women-plus, all attributes vary, but with the taut-muscled bodies of age 18. Small breasts are 46DD. Then I duplicated each, & modified those. Next I merely made 50 copies of all 20. They are the population of Prisma.*
>
> *Nine hundred are Betas, sadomasochistic born servants. All of the other 100 are Alphas, all sadistic. Twenty of those are ravening beast-sadists. Ten of those are plus-Alphas, superbosses with medieval titles. As you will see, I have mingled technology & a medieval-barbaric culture.*
>
> *Clothing is manufactured underground by my computer system—randomly from every fabric & every era. My own creation of subcutaneous dye is used in a number of ways. For one thing, the legs of few Prismans match their skin!*
>
> *Because of my computer control—& my whimsical nature—reality changes on Prisma!—and IS reality.*

The series *Jera* takes its title from the name of a blue-skinned alien with vacant pink eyes and an elongated bald head. She combs through *Playboy, Playgirl, Penthouse,* and *Cosmopolitan,* culling a list of women, then feeds their attributes into a "computrex." The top twenty-seven are kidnapped and modified through serum and surgery. The 187 pages of *Jera* contain the most lavish and intricate use of color. The genius alien finds a planet whose inhabitants have reached the medieval level, and kills everyone with a plague. She then distributes her three thousand creations among the existing city-states, organizes a social hierarchy, and teaches them fetish bondage. Time continues to progress swiftly. The story leaps ahead fifty years, then a hundred, and lands in the three hundredth year. Every so often, all the male children are murdered. Matrilineal royal dynasties rule each city-state of warriors. A new term emerges, a "penoid," or a penis on a female.

The most original comic is entitled *Null-A,* a philosophical term meaning an absence of Aristotelean logic. The two-hundred-page series opens with a lab assistant hopping into an experimental matter transmitter to escape a rapist. She arrives on a foreign planet. By page ten, she's dead of multiple stab wounds. The text says:

> *Epitaph? Perhaps: she came a long, long way for no reason to die for no reason.*

Another comic is subtitled *The Most Awful Tortures Ever Told . . .* A bound woman is nailed to a block of wood and pierced by hundreds of pins, including in her face and eyes. Her left leg is sawed off to reveal a protruding bone. The female killer washes away the blood in order to gloat over the corpse as she masturbates herself to orgasm. A victim is staked spread-eagle in the desert, her bosom doused with honey. A team of "super ants" chews off her breasts, depicted in a series of dramatic panels. Four hours later only her skeleton remains. Another story ends with a very large-breasted woman bound in a hog-tied position, ankles and wrists locked behind her back. She is suspended on a chain. Her captors slowly lower her until only her bosom enters a cauldron of boiling fat. After her breasts fry, they are eaten in front of her.

Throughout history, people have turned up their noses at pornography, dismissing it as disgusting and immoral. I tried very hard to resist such a response. These comics were Dad's most personal work and therefore deserving of careful examination. Looking at them made my stomach hurt. I could peruse them for only short periods before turning away. Despite my revulsion, I felt a horrified sympathy for anyone who lived with such imagery on a daily basis. That it was my own father made it worse. He didn't collect these books, he *made* them. Here was the world he carried inside himself at all times—filled with pain and suffering. I had no idea how miserable he had truly been.

My initial abhorrence gave way to the reckless anger of a teenager. I wanted to lash out at the world, drink and take pills, nullify all that I thought and felt. I became mad at myself for deliberately studying the evidence of what had soiled my childhood. While the family tiptoed around the house to prevent disturbing him, he sat in his office and entertained himself in an appalling manner. I was angry at being raised by a maniacal father and a passive mother with no means of extrication except walking dirt roads until they turned to blacktop. Perhaps my siblings had been right all along—I should've destroyed everything, not out of embarrassment but for the sake of my own mental equilibrium.

It's extremely rare for anyone, let alone a son, to have access to another person's private and unfiltered fantasies. I expected to gain insight through seeing maturity and growth, but the world of Valkyria didn't change. My father never tired of the material and repeated it until he died. By the end—not of Valkyria's saga but of my father's life—plot vanished completely. The pages evolved to single-panel illustrations of garishly colored women enduring profound misery and pain. Text was scribbled haphazardly in available space, with occasional dialogue commenting on the agony of the victim.

Unfettered by market, my father was free to explore all facets of his imagination in *Valkyria*. There was no evolution of character or story, just a steady move toward the greater defilement of women. The books are grisly and grim. Time travel and advanced technology allowed him to include any content without the stricture of logic, physics, or medical consequences.

He made *Valkyria* solely for himself and never showed it to anyone—not even his wife. The secret will hadn't specified it. The four-thousand-page chronicle of the multiverse represents the deepest core of my father's identity, his life's work. For over fifty years he worked on it, overlapping every other writing project. He tried to quit and he couldn't.

Valkyria has a nihilistic bleakness blended with a child's freedom of expression. Perpetrators feel no guilt and prisoners lack all hope. There is no morality. Life is composed of suffering. Existence has no point. It baffled him in 1963 and it baffles me today.

My father often said that if not for pornography, he'd have become a serial killer. On two occasions he told me the same story. One night in college he resolved to kill a woman, any woman. He carried a butcher knife beneath his coat and stalked the campus, seeking a target. It rained all night. No one else was out. He went home soaked and miserable and wrote a story about a man who invented an invisibility serum and killed women at a YWCA. Dad destroyed the manuscript and castigated himself for using invisibility in such an unimaginative way. For me, the crucial element of this story is a man's impulse to tell it to his son.

Many years later he read a biography of a serial killer who owned bondage magazines at the time of his capture. According to Dad, the details of the killer's childhood were "eerily similar" to his own, including three warning signs: bed-wetting, killing animals, and setting fires. When Dad was about twelve, a cat scratched his sister, and he put the cat on trial, dramatically acting out the roles of prosecutor, defense attorney, and judge. The cat was found guilty and condemned to death. Dad hanged it and watched it die.

The three warning signs are known as the "MacDonald Triad,"

but subsequent research refuted the theory that these propensities are indicators of future violent behavior. The traits are not a recipe for a killer. They are regarded as attributes of a distressed child with poor coping skills who might develop a narcissistic or antisocial personality disorder.

If my father was correct that porn prevented him from killing women, then I should be grateful for its continuing presence in his life. Far better to be the son of a pornographer than a serial killer. But I don't believe my father's theory. The sight of blood, even his own, made him light-headed enough to faint. He was not athletic or strong and therefore was incapable of overpowering most people. He was also a physical coward, having never been in a fistfight. He never struck his children or his wife.

The idea that porn prevented him from killing women was a self-serving delusion that justified his impulse to depict women in torment. Thinking of himself as a serial killer if not for making porn was another fantasy on his part, one that allowed him to surrender completely to his obsessions. He needed to believe in a greater purpose in order to continue his work. Admitting that he liked it was too much to bear.

Chapter Thirty-one

IN THE summer of 2015, two years after Dad died, I moved his entire eighteen-hundred-pound archive to a storage unit at the edge of town. His material had occupied a large area in my house, and I needed the space. I needed my mind back, too.

In the weeks after his death, people often asked what I'd say to him if given the chance, what I wished I'd said before he died. Nothing ever came to mind. But in the past year a single private query has risen again and again: *Why didn't you visit me?* It's hard to predict his response. He'd get angry, using wrath to deflect a subject he didn't like. No matter what answer he might have given, I already knew the reason. It wasn't due to pressing deadlines, economic difficulties, or because he didn't love me. It wasn't personal. He never called on my siblings, went on vacations, or visited his mother in the hospital. The truth was glaringly simple—he wasn't capable. He couldn't leave a world he'd carefully constructed, over which he controlled every facet. Such a journey would have exposed the fragility of his omnipotence.

It was left to me to visit him posthumously. I'm glad I did, although the effort took a toll on me. If I'd known the difficulty, I wouldn't have embarked on the project, but once I began, I felt obligated to carry it through. At a certain point I realized that I was searching, but I didn't know for what. The more I delved, the more I discovered similarities between my father and me, a result that left me dismayed.

Buried in a letter from a porn customer in Europe was surprising information. The man thanked Dad for the gift of my first book, *Kentucky Straight*, and complimented my father on the obvious pride he took in my accomplishments. I reread the sentences several times. It was difficult to comprehend that Dad had considered my work good enough to mail to a stranger. He'd never said anything to me about the book. Perhaps learning of my father's pride was what I'd been seeking all along.

Examining Dad's papers brought up hundreds of memories. Most were sad, and I tried to think of good ones. The year before Dad started working from home, he spent a Saturday afternoon with me. He transformed two empty cardboard boxes into castles, one for him and one for me. He cut drawbridges in the front and made a crenellated rampart on the top. We placed plastic soldiers in key positions to defend our kings. Shallow bowls of water served as moats. Using fingernail clippers for catapults, we launched cigarette butts at each other's castle. The goal was to knock down enemy soldiers. Dad sat on the floor across from me, complimenting my good shots, giving me tips on how to load the catapult. His imagination made the game tremendous fun. I felt important in his company, the object of his intense focus and attention. We set up the soldiers and knocked them down again and again, laughing together.

Dad began working at home and we didn't play the game anymore. As the house became his castle, I spent more time outside. My finest hours were roaming the woods. I liked being alone, but

I was happiest with the pack of boys from our hill, sets of brothers on foot and battered bicycles. I don't recall particular events, only the sense of friendship and loyalty, laughter and acceptance. There were no boundaries. Everyone knew us. We could go anywhere. Nothing could hurt us but the land itself. We had each other. We were free. We were happy.

Acknowledgments

For financial assistance during the writing of this book I am grateful to the Lannan Foundation and the Mississippi Arts Commission.

For other assistance, I thank Beth Ann Fennelly, Scott Temple, Allen Steele, Richard Perez, Earl Kemp, Piers Anthony, Joe and Gay Haldeman, Bob Guccione, Jr., Kathryn York, Nicole Aragi, Peter Borland, Duvall Osteen, Faron Henderson, Randy Henderson, Sonny Henderson, Jodie Offutt, Rita Offutt, Jane Offutt Burns, Jeff Offutt, Scotty Offutt Hyde, Melissa Offutt, Sam Offutt, James Offutt, and Melissa Allee Ginsburg.

Andrew J. Offutt Timeline

1934	Born in Spencer County, Kentucky
1944	Wins Spencer County spelling bee
1939–1950	Lives on farm in log cabin
	Teaches self to type and writes two novels
	Begins drawing fetish comic serials
1949	Begins creating *Cade of the Galactic Patrol*, comic serial
1950	Moves to Taylorsville, Kentucky
1951	Wins Kentucky high school fiction contest with "The Devil's Soul"
	Graduates Taylorsville High School one year early
	Enrolls at the University of Louisville on full academic scholarship from the Ford Foundation
1952	Creates *Marcus Severus*, comic book set in ancient Rome
1953	Death of father, Andrew J. Offutt IV
	Resigns from AFROTC; unable to fly due to color-blindness

Uses "Uncle Andy" as byline for *The Cardinal,* school newspaper

1954   Wins *If* magazine college science fiction contest with "And Gone Tomorrow," first professional publication

Applies for job as fetish artist for *Bizarre* magazine, rejected

Returns to drawing *Cade*

Designs ad layouts for Logan Furniture in Louisville

Uses "Morris Kenniston" as byline, referred to as "debut of alter ego"

Writes *The Messenger of Zhuvastou,* published almost twenty years later

1955   Graduates University of Louisville with BA in English

Works at Bonds Clothing for Men in Louisville, Kentucky

Moves to Pikeville, Kentucky, as traveling salesman for Procter & Gamble

Continues drawing fetish serials

1956   Drafted by U.S. Army, fails physical due to asthma

Completes book seven of *Cade*

1957   Moves to Lexington, Kentucky, for promotion with Procter & Gamble

Meets Mary Joe McCabe at a Catholic Youth Organization dance

Destroys all drawn and written fetish material except *Cade*

Marries Mary Joe McCabe

1958   Birth of first child, Christopher John Offutt

1959   Draws two serials for Irving Klaw, rejected

Begins work on *Valkyria,* long-running comic serial

1960   President of the Lexington Toastmasters Club

	Contributing editor for *Moonbeams,* periodical for Procter & Gamble
1961	Birth of second child, Andrew J. Offutt VI
1962	Birth of third child, Mary Scott Offutt
	President of Big Brothers of Lexington, Inc.
	Moves to Morehead, Kentucky, as salesman for Coastal States Life Insurance
	Joins Kiwanis Club
1963–1965	Creates *Nellie, the Farmer's Daughter,* ninety-page fetish serial
1964	Moves to Haldeman, Kentucky
	Birth of fourth child, Melissa Jane (Joe) Offutt
	Starts insurance agency, andrew j. offutt associates
1967	Letter to Pope Paul VI, resignation from Catholic Church
	Writes personal credo
1968	Publishes first novel, *Bondage Babes,* under the name Alan Marshall
	Expands insurance agency to Winchester and Lexington, Kentucky
	"Population Implosion" included in *World's Best Science Fiction*
	Buys a Mercedes-Benz, the only one in Rowan County
	Writes more than a quarter million words in five months
	Sets personal record by writing ninety-four pages in two days
1969	Attends first science fiction convention
	First use of John Cleve as pseudonym on *Slave of the Sudan*
	Acquires first literary agent
1970	Closes insurance agency to become full-time writer

Publishes *Evil Is Live Spelled Backwards,* first science fiction novel

Records seven one-hour tapes for a radio station, "The Writer Speaks"

Writes *Autobiography of a Sex Criminal,* never published

1970–1978 Writes and publishes eighty-eight pornographic novels under multiple pen names

1972 "For Value Received" included in *Again, Dangerous Visions,* anthology heralding the new wave of young SF writers

First use of Turk Winter as pseudonym

1974 Toastmaster at World Science Fiction Convention

1975 Begins long-term collaboration with Eric Stanton

Elected treasurer of Science Fiction Writers of America (SFWA)

1976–1978 Two-term president of SFWA

1977–1979 Edits five volumes of *Swords Against Darkness,* anthology of fantasy

1978 Reveals himself as John Cleve at Kubla Khan VI in Nashville

1982–1985 Creates *Spaceways,* a nineteen-book series, for Playboy Enterprises

1984 Death of mother, Helen Spanninger Offutt

1985 Writes will

Writes "secret will"

John Cleve retires

1986 Emergence of Turk Winter as primary pseudonym/persona

Receives Phoenix Award for lifetime service to Southern SF fandom

1987 Begins Winterbooks to publish his own work

ANDREW J. OFFUTT TIMELINE

1993   Publishes *The Shadow of Sorcery,* last novel

1999   Death of Eric Stanton, best friend and long-term
            collaborator

            Suffers a heart attack, requiring triple bypass surgery

2001   Begins last book of *Valkyria*

2004   Publishes "Dark of the Moon," last short story

2004–2013   Writes novellas for international clientele

            Continues work on *Valkyria*

2013   Dies of acute alcohol-induced cirrhosis

Andrew J. Offutt Bibliography

1951
"The Devil's Soul" (unpublished contest winner)

1954
"And Gone Tomorrow"

1959
"Blacksword"

1966
"Mandroid" (with Robert E. Margroff and Piers Anthony)
"The Forgotten Gods of Earth"

1967
"Population Implosion"
"Swordsman of the Stars" (with Robert E. Margroff)

1968
Bondage Babes
Swapper Town
Sex Toy

Gang Swap
The Seductress

1969
"The Defendant Earth"
The Sex Pill
Virgin Isle
Slave of the Sudan
Nero's Mistress
Bruise
The Seduction of Mary Lou

1970
"Ask a Silly Question"
"The Book" (with Robert E. Margroff)
"Symbiote"
Evil Is Live Spelled Backwards
Barbarana
Jodinareh
Mongol!
Fruit of the Loin
Black Man's Harem
Call Me Calamity
Captives in the Chateau de Sade
The Devoured
The Juice of Love
Swallow the Leader
Seed
Danger: W.O.M.A.N.

1971
"My Country, Right or Wrong"
The Great 24-Hour Thing
Pussy Island
The Second Coming
Pleasure Us!
Rear Entry
The Balling Machine

Four on the Floor
A Miss Guided
Hottest Room in the House
Chain Me Again
Chamber of Pleasures

1972

"Sareva, in Memorium"
"For Value Received"
"Final Solution"
The Castle Keeps
Blond Bitch, Black Buck
Family "Secrets"
Snatch Me!
Wet Dreams
A Girl with Taste
Cellar of Degradation
Her Brother Loves Her Best
My Darling Nephew
A Large Loving Family
Behind Her
Diana's Dirty Doings
Family Indiscretions
Peggy Wants It!
The Three of Us
The Wife Who Liked to Watch
Belly to Belly
High School Swingers
Different Positions

1973

"Meanwhile, We Eliminate"
The Messenger of Zhuvastou
The Galactic Rejects
Ardor on Aros
The Palace of Venus
The Sex Doctor
Never Enough

Losing It
Tight Fit
S as in Sensuous
The 8-Way Orgy
Ball in the Family
The Farm Girl & the Hired Hand
The Domination of Camille
Family Secrets
Holly Would

1974
"Black Sorcerer of the Black Castle"
"Tribute" (with Robert E. Margroff)
"Gone with the Gods"
Operation: Super Ms.
Every Inch a Man
Forced into Incest
MANLIB!
The Sexorcist
Serena's Lost Innocence
Vacation in the Erogenous Zone
Whore of La Mancha
The Accursed Tower
The Passionate Princess
The Fires Down Below

1975
"Enchante"
The Punished Publisher
The Governess
The Genetic Bomb (with Bruce Berry)
Sword of the Gael
A Family Ball!
His Loving Sister
Horny Daughter-in-Law
The Domination of Ann
Succulent Lineup
Mother's Four Lovers

Oversexed Shana
Julanar the Lioness
My Lady Queen
Asking for It!
Begging for It!
Family Bonds
A Degraded Heroine
Cellar of Degradation (illustrated)

1976

"The Greenhouse Defect"
Chieftain of Andor
The Undying Wizard
Brother, Darling!
Disciplined!
Triple Play
Beautiful Bitch
The Complete Couple
The Submission of Claudine
In Leather
Streetfighter

1977

"Bladesmen of Serazene"
"Nekht Semerkeht" (with Robert E. Howard)
"Final Quest"
My Lord Barbarian
Sign of the Moonbow
The Mists of Doom
Forced to Please
Rosalind Does It All
Delicious Discipline
Blunder Broad 1
Blunder Broad 2
Blunder Broad 3
Blunder Broad 4

1978

"At the Beach"
"Hero"
"Kismet"
Conan and the Sorcerer
Demon in the Mirror (with Richard Lyon)
The Look of Lust
Her Pleasure Potion
Blunder Broad 5
Blunder Broad 6

1979

"Shadowspawn"
The Iron Lords
The Sword of Skelos
Blunder Broad 7
Blunder Broad 8
Blunder Broad 9
Blunder Broad 10
Blunder Broad 11
The Adventures of Gwendoline
Space Maidens

1980

"Shadow's Pawn"
Eyes of Sarsis (with Richard Lyon)
King Dragon
Shadows Out of Hell
When Death Birds Fly (with Keith Taylor)
Conan the Mercenary
Temple of Terror
Mark of the Master
Nasty Nurses
The Adventures of Gwendoline, Part II
Space Maidens, Part II

1981

"The Vivisectionist"
Web of the Spider (with Richard Lyon)
Blunder Broad 12
Blunder Broad 13

1982

Rails Across the Galaxy (with Richard Lyon)
The Tower of Death (with Keith Taylor)
Of Alien Bondage
Corundum's Woman
Escape from Macho
Satana Enslaved
The Manhuntress
Purrfect Plunder
Master of Misfit
Under Twin Suns
Blunder Broad 14
Vonda Sorrel

1983

The Lady of the Snowmist
In Quest of Qalara
The Yoke of Shen
Star Slaver
The Iceworld Connection
Jonuta Rising!
Assignment: Hellhole
The Slave Owners

1984

"Rebels Aren't Born in Palaces"
Starship Sapphire
The Planet Murderer
The Caranadyne Horde
Race Across the Stars
Lady Beth
Blunder Broad 15

Blunder Broad 16
Blunder Broad 17
Blunder Broad 18
Blunder Broad 19
Blunder Broad 20
Blunder Broad 21
Blunder Broad 22
Attack of the Princkazons

1985
"The Veiled Lady"
King of the Slavers
Blunder Broad 23
Blunder Broad 24
Blunder Broad 25
Blunder Broad 26

1986
"Blowfly"
"Spellmaster"
Saladin's Spy
Blunder Broad 27
Blunder Broad 28
Blunder Broad 29

1987
"Homecoming"
Shadowspawn
The Kinky Killer-Kidnapper Girls
Horror in San Guana
Blunder Broad 30: Bound
Blunder Broad 31: Outraged
Blunder Broad 32: Assaulted
Blunder Broad 33: The Greatest Bondage Movie Ever Told
Blunder Broad 34: Revenge in Ward XXX
Blunder Broad 35: Double Your Pleasure, Double Your Pain

1988

Kyria of Viria: Dungeons of Darkness
Kyria 2: Year of Conquests
Kyria 3: Happy Daze

1989

"Nightwork"
Blunder Broad 36: Hallowe'en Nightmare
Blunder Broad 37: Captive of Castle Frankenstein

1990

Deathknight
Blundie in Blunderland, Part 1
Blundie in Blunderland, Part 2

1991

Bound in Leather
Blunder Broad 38: The Human Toy
Blundie: How Much Can She Take?
The Pride Sisters 1: Gwendoline X4
The Pride Sisters 2: Gwendoline X4
The Pride Sisters 3: Gwendoline X4
Bound in Rubber 1

1992

The Boss: Book I
The Boss: Book II
The Bondage Twins
Anything You Wish
Anything You Wish 2
Blunder Broad 39: Sex Slave
Blundie vs. the Unholy Trio

1993

The Shadow of Sorcery
Brian's Bitch
The Degradation of Jennifer
Wench

Bound in Rubber 2
Bound in Rubber 3
Dungeons of Darkness
Serena 1: Apprentice Slave
Serena 2: Slave in Training
Serena 3: The Natural
Galexeena: Not-so-Superheroine
Galexeena: Milk-Maid

1994

Blunder Broad: Those Goddam Princkazons Again!
Blunder Broad vs. Barbarian Bitch Bikers
Blunder Broad in Alien Bondage
Blunder Broad: Captive of the Princkazons
Blunder Broad: Captive of the Half-Pints
The Adventures of Blunder Broad
Blunder Broad: Bondagette!
Blunder Broad: Turned On!
The Girl in the Iron Mask: A Tale of Dungeons and High-Tech Devices
The Girl in the Iron Mask 2: Lady Merry
The Girl in the Iron Mask 3: Sib
The Girl in the Iron Mask 4: Tory
The Girl in the Iron Mask 5: Alixi
The Girl in the Iron Mask 6
The Girl in the Iron Mask 7
The Girl in the Iron Mask 8
The Avengers 1
The Avengers 2
Silky 1: Forced Bondage Model
Silky 2: Bondage Model
The School for Womanly Behavior
Punished Teens
The Chronicles of Stonewall Castle 1: Dungeon of Stonewall
The Chronicles of Stonewall Castle 2: Mistress of Stonewall
The Chronicles of Stonewall Castle 3: Punishment of Stonewall
The Chronicles of Stonewall Castle 4: Disciplined in Stonewall
The Chronicles of Stonewall Castle 5: Slave of Stonewall
The Chronicles of Stonewall Castle 6: Horror in Stonewall

The Chronicles of Stonewall Castle 7: Captives of Stonewall
The Chronicles of Stonewall Castle 8: Prisoners of Stonewall
The Little Blonde Girl
The Big Brunette Pony Girl
Michelle's Deserved Degradation 1
Michelle Enslaved 2
Horror Castle
Sweet Gwendoline: The Early Years
The Enslaved 1
The Enslaved 2
Man into . . . Woman? The Degradation of Roger
Buns, Boots & Hot Leather
Blunder Broad 40: The Trouble with Nipples
Galaxeena
A Tale of Two Tails

1995
Blunder Broad vs. Psycho Cycle Sluts
Escalation 1
Escalation 2
Escalation 3
Escalation 4
Another Place
The Domain
Getting Even
Sweet Gwendoline: The Early Years 2
Training Debra 1
Training Debra 2
Nipples: The Enslavement of Regine
Nipples 2: Dairy Maid
The Search for Gwendoline
Homebound: Ms. Bitch-Banker
Homebound II
Jim's Girls
Playmaid Island
Pony-Girl Island
The Pony-Girls
Revenge

Galaxeena, Stantoons 86
Crossover
Virgin Defiled!

1996
"Lord General of Nemedia"
Desperately Seeking Master
Lactia
Purgatory
Escalation 5
Gwendoline and the Missing Princess 1
Gwendoline and the Missing Princess 2
Gwendoline and the Missing Princess 3
Castle de Sade 1
Castle de Sade 2: Castle Steel!
Castle de Sade 3: Steel & Pain
Castle de Sade 4: Baroness Steel
Call Me Goddess 1
Call Me Goddess 2
The Training of Heather
Captured in Africa: Black Rapists
Captured in Africa: Arab Owners

1997
Galexeena
Teacher Enslaved 1
Teacher Enslaved 2: Baby Kim
Teacher Enslaved 3: Changed Relationships
Teacher Enslaved 4: Kim-baby
Escalation 6
Dr. Roissy's Breast Clinic 1
Roissy's Breast Clinic 2
The Terrorized Terrorist
How Clint Became Crista
How Clint Became Crista 2
Bobbi Jo

1998

Anna Nicole: Enslaved
Teacher Degraded by Teens
Country Girl
Fallen Angel
An Extraordinary Girl 1: The Story of Gwendoline & Aunty
An Extraordinary Girl 2
Auntie's Girls 1
Auntie's Girls 2
Roissy Clinic 3: The Punishment of Jonelle
Roissy Clinic 4
Buffy the Vampire Fucker
The Debt
Professor Enslaved by Teens!
Baby Doll
Down with Chastity
Flight to Lilliput 1
Slaves of Lilliput 2

1999

Criminal Host
Melinda Ever Victim
Deep Inside Blunder Broad
CCU—The Chastity Control Unit
Sisters in Slavery 1
Sisters in Slavery 2
Gwendoline and Doctor Ben
Our Niece, Gwendoline
The Enforcer I
The Enforcer II
The Enforcer III
The U-Files

2001

Horror in Bumivia
Blunder Broad and the Mad Scientist

2002

"Role Model"
The Mad (?) Scientist

2003

Convicta Criminala 1
Convicta Criminala 2
Bitch
CTF-13, Book 1 (Correctional Facility-13)
Blunder Broad vs. the Scarlet Lady
Blunder Broad in the Hands of the Goddess of Evil
Blundie the Slave

2004

"Dark of the Moon"
The Cinderella Case
CTF-13, Book 2
Blunder Broad and the Alliance of Evil
Wonder Woman: The End

2005

Katrina and Vanessa
Barbi's World 1
Barbi's World 2

2006

CTF-13, Book 3
The Old Dark House
The Lovers 1
The Lovers 2
Dolls
The Agreement
The W.U.A. (women uber alles)
Turning the Tables
Gurlz 1
Gurlz 2
Gurlz 3
Gurlz 4

Gurlz 5
Gurlz 6
Blunder Broad and the Temple of Doom
Blundie Again
Sisters Enslaved
Charlayne
The Institute
Leda
Barbi's World 3
Barbi's World 4

2007
Barbi's World 5
Barbi's World 6

2008
3 Boo + Wasps
Miss American Beauty
Barbi's World 7: Thade's World 1
Barbi's World 8: Thade 2
Barbi's World 9: Thade 3
Barbi's World 10: Thade 4
Barbi's World 11: Thade 5

2009
Barbi's World 12: Thade's World 6
Barbi's World 13: Thade's World 7
Barbi's World 14: Thade's World 8
Barbi's World 15: Thade's World 9

2011
Luhra
Steamship!
Gurlz 7
Gurlz 8
Gurlz 9
Barbi's World 16: Thade's World 10